The Divine Romance

THE
DIVINE
ROMANCE

Gene Edwards

Tyndale House Publishers, Inc.
WHEATON, ILLINOIS

This book was previously published by Christian Books Publishing House, Auburn, Maine.

Library of Congress Cataloging-in-Publication Data

Edwards, Gene, date
    The divine romance : Gene Edwards.
        p.   cm.
    ISBN 0-8423-1092-4
    1. Bible—History of Biblical events—Fiction. I. Title.
PS3555.D924D58   1993
813'.54—dc20   92-33145

Printed in the United States of America

02 01
12 11 10

DEDICATION

With deepest affection

to my oldest daughter,

Lynda

"Imagination has always had

power of resurrection

that no science can match."

Ingrid Bengis

Above all temples
You chiefly prefer
Oh Spirit
The heart upright
and pure.

Instruct me
You who know
For You were present
from the first.

You sat
dove like
With might
and outspread wings
Brooding over
the vast abyss
And made
it pregnant.

Oh Spirit
what in me
Is dark
Illumine.

The prayer of John Milton as he took up
his pen to write *Paradise Lost*

It has been my fondest hope that we might meet again. When last we met it was a drama that we viewed together.

On this occasion, it is a love story. Of all love stories, I find this one unequaled. I trust, at story's end, you might share that view with me.

The places reserved for us are box seats. We shall have what I hope will be the best possible view of this unfolding saga.

Let us hasten in, now, as I see the ushers are about to close the doors. This is not a thing we would want to miss.

Prologue

He was alone.

The first tick of time had never sounded, nor had the unending circle of eternity yet commenced. There were neither things created nor things uncreated to share space with him. He dwelt in an age before the eternals, where all there was . . . was God. Nor was there space for anything else. He was the uncreated. He was the ALL.

In this non-time of so long ago, there was but one life form . . . the highest life.

He was also love.

Passionate, emotional, expressive . . . love.

In this God, dwelling so all alone, there was a paradox: though he was alone, he was also love. Yet there was no *counterpart* for him to love. A love so vast, so powerful, yet, there was no "other than."

Then life pulsated, light blazed in newfound glory as revelation ascended in him, as he cried from within the council of the Godhead.

There can be two!

"I . . . the living God . . . shall have a *counterpart!*"

Exulting in revelation, he consecrated his whole being to this one task: to have . . . *a bride.* For one brief moment the infinite solitude retreated.

But just before he launched his grand design, a very mysterious thing took place *in* God. Deep within the center of his being there occurred an event that no other eye was to see, no other mind to conceive.

A thousand million portions of God burst upward in light. Each of these portions of God ignited into flaming brilliance . . . as if to proclaim that each had been chosen—even *marked off*—for some special, distant destiny. Having marked off these future destinies, the Living God gave himself to making real his highest dream. Unending self-containment would end.

And so he spoke. "Let there *be* . . ."

In so speaking, he relinquished being the All, making room for something other than the All of God. For one brief moment, there was God *and* a great abyss of nothingness.

Never before, and only once since, has there been such a radical change in the history of God. Now, as "Let there be . . ." sounded across the sphere of nothingness, there came a blinding flash that filled that hollow void. Suddenly there was not only the uncreated God . . . there was now something *created!*

Created *light.* A *picture* of God now shared space with God.

He then created a realm of spirituals. Unmeasured,

immeasurable, this realm, like its God, fell *outside* all finite understandings, yet this invisible, spiritual sphere was *inside* him. He called it the heavenly places. Though it was a place *in* him, yet it pleased him to enfold himself and dwell there.

He then created living creatures! He called them messengers. These beings were covered in light that emanated from their spirits, just as their God is covered in the glory of the light of his own being.

His messengers were like him in many ways, but they were also unlike him. They were powerful, but not *all* powerful. They were everlasting, but not eternal. (Unlike God, who moved about at will in eternity past, eternity present, and eternity future, they moved only forward, into eternity future.) They had no counterpart, but they had one another for companionship. But these messengers were entirely *unlike* God in one way. They were *neuter.* He was male. And they could not love. They could *glory,* yes! But they could not love . . . *not* as he loved.

And though he joyed in having these creatures present with him, and though his solitude had at last been broken, *they* had one another. Like had like; kind had kind. But for him, there was no kind after *his* kind.

Speaking aloud once more, the Lord called out to the abyss of nothingness, and nothingness gave way to something. . . . A *visible* realm now burst forth from his word.

He spoke again, and at his word this visible realm swarmed with sparkling lights and circling orbs.

He then stretched forth his hand, and there dropped from his fingertips a small and shapeless mass. "Upon this small grain I shall labor, for it is the place of my supreme purpose in creating."

As he worked, the void mass began to take on symmetry. As he labored, he filled the little ball with things never before imagined.

By the sixth day, the small planet swarmed with wonders. His audience, the accompanying angels, watched him create a wholly different life from them— visible life that could hear, that could fly, that could run, that could even cry aloud. But the most startling sight upon the blue-green ball was this: Everything was *two*.

Furthermore, an astonishing kind of *two* it was! Not one of these creatures was neuter. They were male—that is, *half* were male! The most incomprehensible wonder in the universe was *the other half!* These beings were not neuter, and they were not male. They were something *new* and beyond all comprehension! They were female! Male had a counterpart. Kind after his kind. Counterparts.

Here was a concept so wondrous that angels spoke of it in hushed reverence, and, staring in pristine innocence at their God, they wondered what had provoked him to create living things that came in twos . . . each *he* having a *she!*

And so they stared, and so they wondered, and so they viewed these newly created things, saying,

> *Like us they live and move.*
> *Like us they have kind of their kind.*
> *But, oh, unlike us*
> *They are visible.*
> *Unlike God or angels,*
> *Each has a counterpart.*

And they took note, that now *all* living things had *someone else* . . . except One. God was still . . . alone.

PART 1

Chapter 1

The sixth day of creation was drawing to a close. The Lord had grown quite weary; therefore, the angels were quite surprised to see him plunge into a final act of creation.

"You will clearly grasp what I am about to do, for you are the highest form of life in the *unseen* realm, the supreme creation within the invisibles."

He paused, reached down, and scooped up a small handful of earth. He stared at the soil for a moment, then spoke again.

"From this red dirt I will create the highest form of life within the realm of things *visible*. The creature I am about to bring forth will rule over the material universe just as *I* rule over the spiritual universe."

With those words spoken, the Lord God began to shape, mold, and model the red dirt.

The angels watched, and as they did they whispered to one another. "This one shall be as God is . . . a *he*."

They stared, enthralled, at their Lord's intensity. They noted how deeply the aloneness, so uniquely his, was etched upon his face.

Suddenly, the look on the face of the Creator changed. He was searching for something . . . something in his own being. Slowly he drew that element from out of himself and engraved it upon the clay.

With the last sculpting stroke, he stepped back from the moist sod, allowing the angels to have a full view of his completed work. They gasped in amazement and cried together,

His image! Visible!

Chapter 2

Once more the Lord God bent gently over the sculptured clay. For a moment the face of the Living God and the face carved upon the lifeless clay almost touched.

The Lord God breathed.

Clay nostrils quivered and flared. The wet clay fleshed, stiffened, stirred, and began quietly breathing.

Almost pensively the Lord stepped back. The newest of his creations turned his head . . . and stared for a brief moment at the panorama of celestial beings gathered about. Then, in the most natural of gestures, the rouge-tinted man sat up . . . turned . . . and serenely faced his Sculptor.

With that the Lord approached the model. Again their two faces almost touched, while angels whispered their approval.

"Why, why . . . they are almost like . . . brothers."

Of all the innumerable creatures fashioned by his poetic hand, there was but one of whom it could be said, "The Lord God was thinking of *himself* when he created *this* one."

And, as the angels had surmised, this latest and final creation was male. Not an *it*, therefore not of the angelic species. Visible, therefore of the material realm, yet a far higher form of life than any other being that dwelt in realms visible.

As the angels stood in wonder at this one, the truth declared itself: This creature would rule the earth . . . as surely as the Lord God, in whose image he was so obviously created, rules the heavenlies.

Further, it was noted, this creature—unlike visible animals and invisible angels, but very like God—could love.

And like God, the one called man had no *kind* after his *kind.* Man joined his God as one of but two living things that could love—yet who had no "other" upon whom to pour out that love. Of all the created beings, man was the only male who had no counterpart.

Truly, man was the image of God.

Chapter 3

The seventh day was a day of rest for all creation. The highest activity of the day reached no higher than wonderment.

The eighth day dawned. It was the second *first* day of the week. For the Lord God, this day was to be a day spent in fellowship with his image. It was obvious that they enjoyed one another's company above all others'.

Together the two traversed man's terrestrial domain, wandering across the face of that emerald ball, roaming meadows, valleys, hills. Together they drank in earth's beauty and absorbed its windsong.

And as they went, first one, then the other, would declare, "Ah, this is good."

"Yes, and this . . ."

"And this, too, is good."

But as the day progressed, the conduct of the man became disturbingly strange. He would fix his penetrating gaze upon some distant, misty object and then suddenly bound his way toward it, only to find the lion, the leopard, or the eagle. For a moment his discovery caused his face to fall. He would then slowly turn and murmur, in a pathos that could disquiet a seraph, "Two. They are always two."

The deep restlessness of the man intensified. At length this disquietude of man was addressed by his Lord.

"You have seen a goodly portion of all my creation, and you have seen the portion I have given you to rule. Is there *anything* in all this vast realm which, to your observation, might *not* be good?"

Slowly, and with the greatest deliberation, man cast his eye over his vast and lush domain. The verdict was incontestable. All was good.

Yet, not all.

There was something amiss deep within the man. Something he could not define . . . yet it was there, and he strove to identify it. A silent cry arose from within and chilled his being to the core.

He again faced his Creator, fixing a steady gaze upon the blazing fires within the eyes of God. Neither spoke while eyes exchanged a consortium of emotions—the mutual loneliness, the shared sadness that they alone, among all living things, had touched.

The Lord at last broke the spell of silence.

"Let us see, for a certainty, if all things in my creation are good."

Man, by some spiritual instinct of his inner nature, knew that he was now to call forth all the creatures of earth and name each of them.

The animals came forth, always in pairs, each with his counterpart. The lion pranced before man with his lioness; the proud stallion and the mare; the bull, the cow. Two, always two.

"What is amiss here?" A wild look grew in his eyes as he cried out, "I am Ish! Man! Ruler of this domain. But alone. One, only. Where is *my* counterpart?"

The last pair of animals passed. Man looked frantically about, then broke into a run across valleys and hills until he came to the precipice of a great mountain and began searching the horizon.

"Are you there?" he called. "Are you there?"

He scoured the whole terrestrial ball, then searched the moon and stars above. Slowly, silently, he made his way back into the valleys and to a waiting and very understanding God. Man again fixed his troubled eyes upon the blazing fire within the eyes of God.

"What is it that is not good?" asked Adam.

"I believe you know. Man, it is not good for you to be alone."

For a long time, the young man and a God not old shared in their spirits what no words, mortal or divine, could ever express.

"You are my image. Male. Alone. And it is not good for you to be thus," said the Lord very quietly.

Man searched out the face of God for a long time before he replied.

"I am, as you are. Alone!"

Chapter 4

Unmindful of path or hour, the man began to wander
. . . without purpose or direction. The unbearable ache
within his heart throbbed on. His senses revealed to
him the harsh truth. "I am more alone than if I were the
only living creature in all realms." Time unmeasured
passed. At last, worn and forlorn, he wandered back to
his Creator.

"You are true, as truth you are," spoke the man as
he approached a God whom he now better understood.
"But is there no deed, no act, of God or man that might
bring forth . . . my Ishah? Even for one brief moment, to
see, to touch—something . . . someone . . . like unto me?
May I not, even for an hour, have *my* lioness?"

The Lord heaved a deep sigh as one about to begin
a great and arduous task. "Man, there is a principle
written within the depths of my being that cannot be
rescinded.

"I am one, not two. Indivisible is my life. And you,
man, are a reflection of my essence. Therefore, one also
are you. As I am alone, so are you alone. As indivisible
am I, so indivisible are you. More than one you cannot

be. To change that is to violate the reflection of me, which reflection you are."

Upon hearing this inexorable verdict, a flawless man, standing in the midst of a flawless universe, began to weep. For the first time creation witnessed the exquisite agony of tears of sorrow.

Man raised his face and, speaking between sobs, said, "You are very much like me, are you not?"

"No, not at all," came the Lord's gentle reply. "*You*, man, are very much like me."

As the full meaning of these words slipped into his soul, the man dropped to his knees, his unspeakable sorrow finding expression only in uncontrollable sobs.

At last the man grew still, lifted his face of blended tears and pain to his Maker, and spoke again, in words of grim finality. "There is, then, no way. As you are, so I am destined ever to be."

An overwhelming heart of love and a life lived out in solitude now found a hesitant voice and measured words:

Perhaps, my image,
perhaps
there is
a way,
But only one.

The Creator reached down to the soil and plucked forth a *seed*. For an endless moment, the man watched his Lord stare silently and sadly at the seed.

Slowly the Lord God held out the seed for the man to see.

"Here is yet another principle, buried deep within my nature. This principle, therefore, is found also in the very fiber and bloodstream of the universe. Even in *you*, man. 'Tis a law of my nature, not known to my creation, yet this principle lives also within this small, terrestrial seed. Like us, this simple seed is alone. And—like us—it must *forever* abide . . . alone."

"Forever? . . . my Lord, my God . . . alone . . . *forever?*"

"Yes, man . . . forever . . . *unless* . . ."

"Unless what?" cried the man at this faint hint of hope. "Tell me! Unless *what!*"

"Unless . . ." The Lord paused.

"In the name of pity, unless what!"

The answer came quietly and evenly. "Unless, perchance, the seed should fall into the ground and there cease its existence." With that, the Lord dropped the seed into the earth.

Man rushed to the site of the burial and exclaimed, "But I cannot fall into the ground and cease to exist." He paused, lowered his voice and added, "That is . . . well . . . I cannot, can I?"

The Lord turned and, gazing into some far distant age, murmured, "Perhaps—perhaps one day such a thing might come to pass."

"But," interrupted the still-agitated man, "what would be the good of it?" He stared again at the moist sod. "For what gain would it be if *I* should disappear forever into the earth? Then, should my counterpart appear, my *counterpart* would be *alone.*"

"Have you not observed, man—and I believe you have—that eventually the seed *rises* again. It rises from the captivity of its earthen chamber. And, having risen, the seed is no more *one* seed. And no longer alone. The seed is *many.*

"Yet I tell you a mystery. The seed is still . . . *one.*"

The man stood almost motionless, fixing his eyes first on the earth and then on the face of God. Slowly, but with rising expectation, he replied,

All I have heard
I do not fully see.
Your thoughts are beyond
those bestowed on me.
Your sight is not mine to own.
Nor angels nor archangels, I presume,
have ever known this thought.
But this I declare,
Make me a seed!
Place me now, this hour,
into that dirt
from which I sprang.
Out from your finger
or out from my heart
bring forth to me now
my counterpart.

These words seemed to end, for the Creator, some eternal vigilance of waiting.

"You, my very image, are willing to fall, like this singular seed, into the earth that you might thereby end your journey of solitude? You are willing to do *this* to gain a life from your life? You could fall into the earth and cease to exist in order to become as this seed—*many*. You are willing to do this to have a counterpart?"

The man turned to face his God and exclaimed in a voice of unequivocal certainty.

"I am! I am!"

The Lord God lifted first his eyes, then his hand toward the heavenly realms. The celestial response was immediate.

The heavenly host bolted forth into realms visible. A wild, joyous, and expectant throng they were, encircling their Creator and his highest creation. Soon the two were surrounded with angelic light and praise. In the midst of this celestial demonstration the Lord raised his hand again and roared forth a most thunderous and uninhibited declaration.

"For man," he shouted. "For man, I shall now build a counterpart. Kind after his kind!"

The praise vanished. Stunned, the angelic host stood silent. These were words they did not understand. What God had suggested, they knew full well, was quite impossible.

"This is the eighth day, is it not?" inquired the angels of one another.

"Indeed, it is the eighth day, not the sixth."

"And our Lord declared creation and all creating to have ended on the sixth day, did he not?"

"Can a male bear a child?" came an angelic whisper as yet another probed his inmost being for revelation.

How can the image of God be two, *when God is* one? was the unanswered, unspoken question, burning in the spirits of all the angels.

The Lord turned to face the red-tinted creature standing beside him, that he might answer for them these unanswerable questions.

"You are of the earth. From this very soil I brought you forth, but *not* from this soil shall I bring your counterpart." The Lord paused. Every angel leaned forward. "No, not from the soil . . . but from here!"

Every eye, human and angelic, followed the finger of God. A muffled gasp arose from each and all. The Lord's finger was now, quite clearly, pointing to the man's side.

"Your counterpart is, even now, hidden *in* you!" declared the Lord. "Counterpart shall be not only *for* you, but *of* you and *by* you—of your life, of your substance. Counterpart will be *your* being. She shall be you, extended! Bone of your bone. Flesh of your flesh. Being of your being. Essence of your essence."

"Oh!" exclaimed one of the angels quietly as he tilted slightly to whisper to another. "Then it is not creation at all. It is a building matter, of sorts."

"But what of God's oneness?" asked a still-curious angel.

"How should I know?" came the befuddled reply. "We have been here only since the foundation of the ages and the beginning of time and eternity . . . not *before!*"

The whispering faded. The Lord was staring at man. Slowly he raised his hand and passed it over the face of man.

Again the angels gasped.

Man slipped to the ground and lay very still. Indeed, *too* still.

"Has the inward portion . . . ceased to exist?"

"I believe not, he still glows."

"But how can *anything* be so . . . so still?"

"Let us trust, even in this strange sight, that all things in God's creation are still good."

Now if one thrusts his hand into water, he shall surely bring forth water. And, perchance, if one thrusts his hand into the earth, he shall surely bring forth earth. It follows, then, that should the Living God thrust his hand into the side of man, he would surely bring forth humanity. And this very thing he did, drawing forth from *within* man a portion of that man. A part of the man's own being was now *separated* from man, yet that portion was still of man.

Angels stood dumbstruck, watching man cease to be one, and yet remaining one.

"You see," said the Lord softly, "there is something . . . *someone* . . . hidden *in* Adam."

The Lord brought forth from man's side a bone—a softly *glowing* bone—and held it up for all to see.

"The man is no longer one. He is divided, yet both parts are . . . still that man," declared the Lord.

"Never could I have conceived that such a thing could be," spoke one of the angels to himself. "Truly, there are many wonders to be found in the ways of God."

The Lord God now turned to face the angelic host.

"From this bone, taken from the inward parts of man, I shall *build* his mate."

"He . . ." The Lord's voice trembled. Every angel tensed, a few instinctively reaching for their swords.

"Man . . . shall now have one beside him. One of his very substance, his being . . . extended. I shall now build flesh from his flesh. Bone from his bone. Thus shall he gain a counterpart. A counterpart who is oneness. A counterpart upon whom he may pour out . . . his love."

As one, the angels bowed their faces to the earth. Some small revelation of the unfolding drama had made its way into their spirits. They stood again and began to sing softly as Creator now became Builder.

Soon the singing gave way to silence, for the scene before them enthralled their whole being.

Chapter 5

"Behold, no inconsistency is here," said one of the angels, resuming his quiet inquiry. "In our realm, in the *invisibles*, there are no counterparts. But here in man's realm—in the visible world—*all* things have counterparts. So, it is a natural thing for man also to have a counterpart." The angel rose to his full height, as one about to bring to conclusion a great mystery. "It is a matter of visible or *not* visible. Though man is the image of God, he *is* visible. And God is invisible. Therein lies the difference! Invisible, spiritual . . . no mate. Visible, physical . . . a mate."

"Still," wondered the audience of one that stood beside him, "still, if the *image* can have a mate, why then cannot God—the *original*—have a mate? And besides, man is not *just* of the physical realm. He is partly of the spiritual. He is not wholly like the animals, you know. He glows!"

The whispered conversation ended abruptly.

As the Lord worked, the form of the new being was becoming discernible. Suddenly one of the archangels—the angel of light—moved through the throng and approached the Lord. A murmur of astonishment rose from the heavenly host. That anyone would intrude upon their Lord at such a moment was quite . . . unangelic!

"Might I form in words what each of us has asked within our spirits?"

"You may," replied the Lord.

"You are fashioning for man a counterpart. Will you also create for *yourself* a counterpart?"

Consternation broke out in angelic ranks. Never had such conduct been seen, nor a question so inappropriate been conceived. And, surely, *never* had such a question ever been asked.

The Lord's answer came unnervingly calm.

"Creation is ended. How can I create, when creation is over? No, by the immutability of my own nature, and the sureness of my word, the matter of creating is forever ended."

There was a finality in this declaration that ended all questions.

The archangel relaxed, but all the other angels tensed.

"No," came the Lord's voice, again so calm, so quiet that angels strained to hear. "Neither man nor . . . I . . ." He paused. "Neither man, nor any other, shall have a counterpart from out of this creation. *Creating* has ended. Furthermore, you may mark this hour the last counterpart *this* creation will ever see."

He now turned to address the archangel face to face. "It would necessitate a whole new creation, and therefore the end of this one, to perform so grand a deed. Nor could *I* ever have a *created* counterpart. Kind after my kind would, necessarily, have to be *uncreated*—would it not—for *I* am uncreated! Nonetheless . . ."

The conversation ended. The Lord returned to his work. The archangel, his curiosity somewhat assuaged, returned to his appointed place above the angels, and beside the throne.

Now, more intently than ever, the Builder returned to fashioning the shimmering, glowing form that had been, only moments before, but the rib of a man. Quite abruptly and unexpectedly, he stopped. So perfect was his stillness it chilled the heavenly host. Slowly, at first imperceptibly, the light within the Lord began to brighten. And it grew brighter yet as revelation within him intensified. Angelic alarm broke out as this growing light began to envelop first the angels, then the earth, then the galaxy. Upward, outward the light soared until its brightness had swallowed up all visible creation.

There was no question. Not since the moment when God first conceived of creating had the brightness of revelation known such brilliance.

Still higher—and brighter—the light ascended, pouring into the heavenly places, filling every crevice of the invisible realms. The length and breadth of creation was now swallowed up in the glory of the light of God as he considered this matter of . . . a counterpart!

The angels crumbled in terror before such brightness. Their own spirits, now immersed in God, began to touch the thought of God. They were drowning in bursts of spiraling revelation.

Slowly the revelation subsided, giving angels a moment to wonder what *ultimate* thought had coursed through God's being. What masterpiece might now fall from his hand? At last they could pierce the light and see again the face of God. Upon that face was etched exaltation and joy.

Whispered one angel as he staggered to his appointed place, "He has contemplated man's counterpart. He has *seen* her in the eye of his mind. But somewhere beyond that sight, methinks, he has glimpsed a higher, far greater revelation. But what?"

"'Tis mystery, hidden in unapproachable light," rejoined another.

Now it was with trembling hands that the Builder did build, and mold, and fashion, and mold again. And while the being he fashioned took on its final form, awed and dumbfounded angels fell once more to their knees at the sight of the wonder before them.

One angel, most irreverently, cried aloud the thoughts of all: "He is not making another Ish. This one is alike, yet different. As the lioness is to the lion, so is this *out-of-man*. But never, never," cried the wayward angel, "was lion or lioness so beautiful as this."

Another angel broke the confines of restraint.

"Nor was even man so beautiful as this!" he exclaimed.

With that, the vaults of heaven broke open, and in one full-throated shout, all heavenly beings proclaimed:

Never was
nor e'er shall be
as beautiful
a thing as she.
All hosts in
heaven's court,
all creatures on
earthen sod,
it matters not
the tribe nor race,
one sight alone can
be
more beautiful than
she.
It is the face
of God.

Chapter 6

"I am sure I understand it now."

"And what is that?"

"The light . . . the light that a moment ago almost consumed us! Our God cannot have a counterpart; nonetheless, he saw within his eye what she might be . . . *if* ever she could exist . . . *the counterpart of God.* By revelation he saw what she would be if he had an Ishah! Then he held that vision before him, a vision of *his own mate* . . . and then fashioned the bone of man into a counterpart. Do you not realize! This *she* is fashioned in the image of his vision of his own counterpart! The mate of man is a picture of that counterpart of God, which God will never have."

"If this one formed by the hand of God is an image, ah, then what might God's counterpart be, if indeed she could be!"

"'Tis a thing we shall never know."

"Nor shall our God."

"It is no wonder then," continued the angel, "that having completed this supreme masterpiece—as I am sure you noted—our Lord knows but a melancholy joy."

Chapter 7

The Lord stepped back from the pulsating form that all might see her. A living, breathing creature lay quietly at his feet, robed in an iridescent glow. She appeared as one who might have been chiseled out of sunlight.

For a long moment the angels gazed at this wholly new being whose form, contour, and features were beyond all imagination to conceive or mind to capture.

Here was a counterpart to man, kind after his kind. And now—all knew—there could be sons of man and daughters of man . . . after *his* kind.

Man—the image of God—having "after his kind" was a thought that had never before crossed their spirits.

It was *out-of-man* who broke the angelic spell. She opened her eyes and looked curiously about. As she rose, a cry of delight issued from the angels as they beheld such regal grace. At last her eyes fell upon the face of God. She tilted her head slightly, as curiosity gave way to wisdom.

"Thou art my Lord, my Creator and my God."

"I am," came the Lord's soft reply.

She cast her eyes far across the celestial host, then turned again to her Lord.

"There is but *one* of you," she observed.

Then, smiling, she gestured toward the angels.

"There are *many* of you.

"And I . . . am I but one? Or am I many?"

The answer came as quickly as it came surprisingly, for it came in but one word.

"Go," said the Lord, pointing in a direction quite opposite from where the man lay sleeping.

"Go. Beyond the angels. Beyond the animals. To the hills. To the mountains. Go, and there await."

The woman stretched out her hand and touched the hand of God, then turned and disappeared into the west.

The Lord turned and moved toward the east. The angels followed, their thoughts all one.

"She was in man. She was hidden right there, in him! Unseen, unconceived of . . . by any mortal mind. Yet there she was, all the time, *in* him. She was an unrevealed mystery hidden *in* man.

"And the Ancient of Days, we know him well, yet not at all.

"Long before we came, what other mystery might there have been?

"What thing, what glorious *mystery* might yet be hidden *in* him?

"A counterpart *in* God? Kind after his kind? Being

of his being? Nature of his nature? And . . . sons of God!
And daughters of God!

"Could it be that hidden in God is a . . . No! Of
course not. The thought is unthinkable!"

Chapter 8

The Lord gazed intently at the opening in man's side. Time seemed to move forward before his eyes. He was looking upon some distant scene no other eyes could see. Sadness fell across his face as he knelt down before the quiet, still form of the man.

"So this is the way it is . . . and shall be," he said, almost in a moan. Tenderly he closed the wound—the wound from whence had come *man's* counterpart.

The Lord then whispered to the motionless form before him. "Once you were one, yet a great mystery was in you. Now you are two. But as is my nature, so is yours. You must soon be *one . . . again!*"

Man opened his eyes, and with the first instant of consciousness he frantically grabbed his side. His eyes widened.

"Hallelujah!" he exclaimed. "Something is missing!"

He sprang to his feet and whirled about, exclaiming, "Where is she! Where is my out-of-man?"

"Man," responded a calm but much ignored Lord, "I would walk with you for a moment."

"Yes! Yes! But where is she?"

The Lord waited.

Man dropped his hands, turned toward the Lord, and smiled. "You have made angels swift, yet your ways are sometimes slower even than mine!" With that he joined his Lord, and together they walked.

"Your substance has been divided, man. Yet it remains the same. She is of you, out of you, from you, and one with you . . . yet now separate.

"You are, and ever shall be, my image. Therefore she must return to you, this substance of your substance. She must become, once more, *one* with *you.*"

"I do not fully understand all that you have said," replied the man slowly.

"It is not necessary that you understand. But it is important that you pour out your love on her. For now, at last, your love has somewhere to go."

Betraying some hidden doubt, man responded, "I have never expressed this love that beats within me. Will I . . ."

"I have fashioned from your being a *she.* And, yes, you will know how to express that love that is now still captured within you."

"And . . . and then?"

"Counterpart will, of course, return that love to you."

The man stopped. "You mean," he responded, stunned at the idea now coursing through him, "you mean that love shall not only be given, but shall also be *received?* Love will be returned?"

The Lord's own being trembled at the word. "Yes. Given . . . *and* received," he replied.

Turning to fix his full gaze upon the face of God, the man inquired, "And what shall such an experience be likened to, to receive love from *an other than* . . . to receive love from a counterpart?"

A deep look of sadness crossed over that incomparable face.

"There resides in the council of my being an exchange of fellowship . . . and of love about which you know nothing. *Within* my being courses a love of Fatherhood and Sonhood . . . of which you are but a reflection. The depth and breadth of *this* love is beyond all mortal conception. But the love of a counterpart . . . this is a matter of discovery you will know and I shall never. . . . It is a matter you will know *before* I know!

"Now, wait here. Wait, until you see . . . or hear."

With those words the Lord disappeared.

Chapter 9

To fill the vacancy of her solitude, she had wandered deep into unexplored places, pausing now and again to admire the handiwork of her Lord's creation. The ocean of aloneness that surrounded her, nonetheless, began to engulf her whole being.

An outward cry of despair, to give expression to some inward longing, was about to rise from her throat when the Lord suddenly appeared before her. For a long moment he studied the deep loneliness so evident upon her face.

"Is there something here in my creation that is not good?" inquired the Lord.

"My Lord, my God, my Creator, this creation is beautiful beyond all explaining. But I am here, all alone."

"Yes, I know. I, too, have dwelt in aloneness for a very long time."

"Shall I ever be alone? Am I the only one of my kind?"

"I shall answer that question now," replied the Lord. "I will summon all earthly creatures to this place."

With that, he raised his hand. Far away, all animals of all kinds turned to face the west.

As the multitude of beasts swarmed across the horizon, they gradually formed a vast circle around their Lord and the beautiful creature beside him.

"Always they come by two," she observed quietly.

"Gaze carefully upon them, Eve, and as you do, listen to the spirit within you."

Instantly Eve sensed, for the first time, a place within her . . . some deep, hidden, *spiritual* place. And with that discovery she laid hold of a whole new realm of her being. Revelation burned within her.

Now the revelation gave way to utterance.

"All things here are in their proper order. Yet something of my life is *not* in order."

As the last animal passed before her, she again faced her Creator, yet no word was uttered.

The Lord raised his hand and pointed toward a distant place, and with that the two began the ascent of a very high mountain.

"I am beautiful," said Eve at last, speaking in a childlike innocence. "Perhaps more beautiful than any of the other creatures. Thou hast made me so. And I can love. No . . . I *do* love. But there is none to love."

She stopped abruptly.

"I am a lioness, yet there is no lion."

With a faint note of joy slipping into his words, the Lord responded, "Truly, you are an incredible creature." Then smiling softly, he added, "And, yes, I have made you so! You are perfect, Eve. As perfect as anything *created* can be perfect. Nor can you—or any other creature—reach beyond your present perfection, except you take into yourself that which is *not created.*"

"I understand not, my Lord."

"It is *divinity* alone that is *truly* perfect," he replied.

"But you have not answered my question, Eve. Is there anything in my creation that is not good?"

The woman paused, struggling with the question, seeking to form an answer. Suddenly a smile broke across her face.

"But, my Lord, I cannot answer your question until you have answered mine. Am I alone, or is there another like unto me?"

"What joyful company you will make for your mate . . . if such a mate exists!" replied the Lord with a delighted laugh.

"Does one?" she queried again.

"Eve, you are not alone. Yes, there is one like you. And . . . Eve . . . he waits, even now, for you.

"Go! Go, and find him."

With those words the Lord once again disappeared.

And Eve whispered, "Then, my Lord, I will answer your question. Yes! All things *are* good."

Chapter 10

She moved in an ever-widening circle, sometimes traversing meadows, sometimes climbing hills, but always searching. The intense longing within her heart grew with every passing hour. But always, there was no *he* to be found.

In desperation she stretched her hands toward the heavens and cried, "Where is he? Where is my *he?*"

She heard again the words of her God: "Listen to the spirit, deep within you."

With that, the spirit within her leaped. The soft glow that covered her shone now in almost angelic intensity. She sensed the air, and there, on the highest of mountains, called forth the ends of her strength to cry aloud.

"Lord! Lord Adam! Come! Come, Lord Adam. Come quickly!"

Once more she sensed the air about her. Once more the glow of her spirit leaped outward in renewed brightness. Whirling about toward the east, she began running with all her might.

Chapter 11

Far beyond the distant horizon, upon another mountain, a weary and saddened man shot to his feet, turning westward as he did. Something within his spirit had leaped. He glowed now with a light that surely matched any angel's.

"She is there. Somewhere. I sense her. She is calling. For *me!*"

Consumed with excitement, he plunged down the mountain, leaping streams, circumventing boulders, and vaulting rills. There was near madness in his westward plunge.

He was certain now. She was near, and she, too, was moving . . . toward him . . . and with the same abandon.

Never before, never since, has a man moved so swiftly. The very air whistled in his path.

Across plain and meadow she came, hesitating only long enough to sense again the deep instincts of her spiritual being. Then she bolted forth again to press the laws of nature in her speed.

Unknown to either, their paths would meet at the very entrance to the Garden of Eden.

For one bright instant, though still far away, he glimpsed her. "I saw her. She is out there. I saw her! A lighted figure, like unto me. I saw her, but she has disappeared." Once more he lunged into flight.

Then, in a far-distant place, this time not with spirit but with ear, he heard, "Come, Lord Adam, come!"

Half mad he leaped toward the echo of the sound, fairly screaming:

Behold, I come! I come!

Out from behind one of the vast roots of the Tree of Life, the glowing figure appeared again! He could see her clearly now, more beautiful than anything his imagination had ever conceived. She disappeared again from view, leaving the man quite at the end of sanity.

"My she, my she!" he cried, half running, half stumbling. Surely she had seen him, he thought. "And she matched me in flight. She desires to come to *me!*" With that he found himself not only running and weeping, but thundering,

I love you. I love you. Do you hear? I love you!

She came once more into view. The space separating them was closing fast. Each halted very suddenly, not at all sure what next to do. Then man roared again, "Do you hear? I love you!" Spontaneously, they flew into one another's arms as he heard her unequivocal reply. "I love you, too. I love you . . . as you love me."

With joy, with shouts, with laughter, and with tears, they clung to one another in wild embrace, yet all the while the man continued to cry, "You are beautiful. More beautiful than archangels. And I love you, I love you."

As she could, she replied, "And I love you, too."

Laughing in quiet delirium and exulting in uninhibited joy, he released his embrace and held her high in his mighty arms. He threw back his head and bellowed to the heavens,

> *I love!*
> *At last, I love.*
> *And love has been returned.*

With the excitement of a child, he held her at arm's length and cried again, quite beside himself, "Did you know? Did you know that you were once in *me?* Hidden *in* me! Here. See! You! Such a beautiful creature as you. *In me.* Right here in my side. That is where you were. And did you know—you are made . . . of *me!* We . . . were . . . separated. Now look at us. We are together again. You have returned to me!" He pulled her toward him, whirling about as he did.

"Together. Forever!"

His final words seemed to roll across creation.

Now holding her beside himself, he glanced

quickly around, then raised his hand toward the heavens.

> *Creator, Lord.*
> *Hear me!*
> *Angels, hear me!*
> *Seraphim and cherubim.*
> *Creatures of the deep,*
> *upon the land,*
> *and in the sky.*
> *I am* ***one*** *once more.*
> *Behold, my counterpart!*
> *More beautiful, more glorious*
> *than all realms combined.*
> *At last!*
> *Bone of my bone,*
> *flesh of my flesh.*
> *And I . . . man!*
> *Your earthen lord . . . I . . .*
> *I . . . am . . . no . . . longer . . . alone!*
> *Hear me,*
> *realms seen.*
> *Hear me,*
> *realms unseen.*
> *The aloneness is broken*
> *forever!*
> *And now, my Lord,*
> *my God,*
> *my Creator—*

It was not good for
man
to be alone.
*And I am **not** alone.*
Henceforth,
forever,
All things are good.

"There remains but one thing, the ultimate completion of all oneness—first . . . *you* in me, now . . . *I* . . . in you!"

So it came about, there in the serene beauty of the Garden of Eden, a place more beautiful than heaven and earth, he embraced her again. And while angels rejoiced in that primordial age of innocence, the ruler of earth and his counterpart became, once more . . . one flesh.

Chapter 12

Unnoticed by any created eye, the Lord God quietly withdrew. While angels broke forth in exultation at man's joy, the Lord rose above the earth, above the sky. He returned to heavenly realms, and yet again he ascended. Above and beyond even heavenly realms, he rose. Back to that nonplace, outside time, outside eternity . . . back to where he was the *All*.

There, utterly alone, as alone he had so long been, the Lord God released from the depths of his heart a cry of sorrow.

No. No!
Man!
*All things are **not** good.*
It is not good
that God
should be alone!

Chapter 13

There are angels more curious than others, and the afternoon of the eighth day found two of the more curious musing over the events of the morning.

"There is much I do not fully comprehend."

"Such as . . . ?"

"The woman was *in* the man. True?"

"As we both bore witness!"

"And man is the image of God, is he not? Then is there something that is even now *in* God?"

"You are asking me?"

"I am. And I am asking you yet another matter. Man and his counterpart, were they not united again—once more utterly *one*? And was it not true that there, in the garden, he was *in* her?"

"So it was."

"And man is the physical and visible image of an invisible God! Is he not a physical *picture* of spiritual reality?"

"You have already asked that question once," replied the other.

"Well, to the point. Is it not possible that one day,

in the realms of the *spirituals*, the Lord God might also be *in* something . . . or someone . . . who was first hidden *in* him. That one, in him. He, in that one?"

"I suppose, *if* there is someone now hidden in God, then it might follow that one day God shall be hidden in that someone! Perhaps. I do not know. I am, after all, only an immortal angel."

Chapter 14

The Lord extended an invitation to the man and woman to make their abode in Eden, the very Paradise of God.

Often they walked with him there, and as they did, they spoke with him of many things. But on occasion he withdrew—that is, from *their* view. In a distant place he would watch—and consider the ways of this living image of himself.

"They are never distracted from one another, for there is no distraction. In their eyes, nothing else exists!

"She has no blemish; she has no wrinkle. There is nothing imperfect in all her being.

"He loves her continuously. And with abandoned, innocent, unbridled passion, she loves him in return.

"She has full confidence in her place beside him. No reassurances need be given that he loves her. She never questions, but totally accepts his love. There is no fear of displeasing him or losing him.

"She is beautiful, she knows that, yet there is no pride. Rather, a deep inward knowing that he is lord of all earth, and she is . . . his perfect mate."

The Lord God turned and moved away. But not before he smiled and whispered to himself:

*And when that wondrous
day arrives, so shall these
things be true . . . of my Eve.*

PART 2

Chapter 15

He had stood there all morning, high upon the summit of a great desert mountain, watching intently toward the south. Finally, in late afternoon, it began to appear, first as a tiny speck on the horizon, gradually growing until it became a moving sea of humanity. It was *his* people, lately set free from slavery.

Tomorrow, he knew, he would meet with their leader on this very mount and speak to him face to face of many things that weighed upon his heart.

For a moment, though, his thoughts wandered back to the Garden of Eden, to the disobedience, to the horrible fall of man and the fall of all creation. He recalled again the flood and Noah. The water had hardly receded when the cycle of failure had commenced yet again.

Today he would begin once more. And what would be the outcome?

The fleeing refugees were coming into clear focus now. He could make out Moses in the lead, the mohair tents, the cattle and sheep, even the vague outline of his people. He stared at this moving mass of humanity until the image before him blurred and began to change in form and, finally, became but one person. His eyes now saw not a multitude of people, but only a lovely young girl, coming up from Egypt, crossing the hot sands and moving toward him.

"She will be here by evening. Soon she will enter the land I have promised to her. There she will reach full womanhood. I have waited since before eternity. I have created the whole reaches of the cosmos for but this one Purpose.

"I wonder . . . I wonder. Will she learn to love me?"

Chapter 16

Though he was well over eighty now, the man moved with a quick and sure foot as he mounted a huge rock around which a million people were gathered. They had come, on this grand occasion, to hear him speak. Slowly, but in a loud, clear voice, he began to recount to them the tale of their long and venerable history, bringing again to their minds the miraculous events of the last few days.

"After the great flood, when all mankind was destroyed because of their wickedness and because they had forgotten their God, the family of Noah again brought forth children. Once more the race of man covered the earth, and once again the sons of man turned from their God and filled the earth with their iniquity.

"For the second time the Lord God repented that he had made man. He gave them up. Once more he called forth a single family to follow him. Today, all about you, you see the descendants of that family. A nation has come forth from Abraham, Isaac, and Jacob.

"Today the Lord God has called this people to

return to the land where once dwelt our ancestor Abraham. Upon that land, and from that land, we are destined to live.

"It is to *you* that the Lord has turned his great love. But be not proud. For it is not that you are a fair and noble people that he loves you. No! For you are the sons and daughters of slaves, a people despised. Nor is it because you are a great and large nation that he loves you. No! For you are the smallest of all nations.

"Then why does he love you?

"He loves you . . . because he loves you.

"Today we journey once again toward that land that the Lord gave to our father, Abraham. When you have entered that land, you will grow strong and prosper. In *that* day, do not forget your God. Turn not to the ways of the nations surrounding you. Fill that land with iniquity as other nations fill theirs, and you will surely learn the Lord's displeasure. Even his wrath.

"Remember his mercy to us, his faithfulness in the land of Egypt and beside the sea. Had it not been for his mercy, that sea would surely, even now, be our grave.

"And what is it the Lord asks of you . . . this day . . . and in the day you enter the land he has promised to you?

"I have stood before him, face to face. I have seen his holiness . . . yet lived! I have watched his power . . . unlimited. I have drowned in his glory . . . indescribable. What does such a God require of us? But one thing. Above all else, *one* thing." Moses paused, then cried out,

> **Love him**
> *With all your might.*
> *Love him*
> *With all your mind.*
> *Love him*
> *With all your soul.*
> *Love him*
> *With all your being.*
> *Love him!*

Chapter 17

As the great throng broke up, the words of Moses still ringing in ears and hearts, the people returned thoughtfully to their tents. And as they gathered in those dwellings, they shared their hearts.

Among one family, of the tribe of Levi, there occurred this conversation.

"Oh, father, I do love him. I wish to serve him. This very day I shall speak with Aaron. I wish to devote my whole life to serving our wondrous Lord . . . his dwelling . . . and his people."

A short distance away, a wife turned to her husband, searched his face for a moment, and then spoke her heart.

"Oh, husband. In Egypt ours was a lot far easier than most of our countrymen. And the gifts given us upon our departure were no small things, for either slave or free. I see in your eyes that your thoughts are mine. Our God is so gracious, so kind, and we do love him, with all our hearts. All that we have of silver and gold, let us give to him."

Quick and eager was the husband's response.

"Yes, with a heart of love, let us give him such as we have."

And in another tribe, far distant from the Levites, a group of fervent young men spoke in grave and measured words.

"It is agreed. Today, here and now, we make a solemn vow to our Lord and to one another. We will forever obey the voice of our God. What he speaks we will do. Always. Whatever he asks, be it a small thing or be it our very lives, we will obey the voice of the Lord. If he speaks in the silent places of our hearts or in the hearing of our ears, or be it to Moses that he should speak, his demand shall instantly be our will, as long as breath is in us."

"'Tis not enough," broke in another. "Prayer! Let us covenant to pray. To be men of prayer, upon our knees, seeking his face, allowing him to search our hearts. Yes, and asking for power to do his will in hours of need and crisis."

As they spoke of these things, an elder of the tribe rushed by, hurriedly seeking out the other leaders of his tribe. Having found them, he spoke in fervent terms.

"This we must do! Tomorrow let our tribe assemble. Let us come with our cymbals and trumpets. Behold—here in my hand—already a song has been written by one of our youth. 'Tis a psalm exhorting us to extol the ways of our God. Let us take this song and other psalms of praise; let us render them unto our Lord and fall down upon our faces and worship him to-gether."

Eagerly the elders agreed, "Surely there is no bet-ter way to show our love for our God than to pour out our worship before him."

By nightfall the great rock upon which Moses had spoken was vacant, except for one lone figure. Unob-served by all, he had been there listening—listening to Moses recount to the people his very own message to them. Afterward he had walked among his people, listening intently to their every word.

A deep sadness now disturbed the face of the Lord, for he was contemplating the response he had heard from his people.

A long, deep groan of sorrow, unheard by human ears but shattering the tranquility of the entire heavenly host, rose up from his depths.

I did not require of you
your wealth nor coins of gold.
What need have I of these?
I did not ask of you
that you serve me.
Do I, the Mighty One,
need to be waited upon?
Neither did I ask of you
your worship nor your prayers
nor even your obedience.

He paused. Once more a long, mournful groan rose from his breast.

I have asked but this of you,
that you love me . . .
love me . . .
love me.

Chapter 18

In the eyes of earthen man she was a nation, but through the eyes of God she was a woman. A nation, yes, but in his sight a composite woman who foreshadowed his bride. He also knew what no angel nor man knew—nor even dreamed: Out from her would one day come his bride. Therefore he loved this one, visited her, counseled her.

There were those who vied for her love and who sought to embrace her. There were also those who would destroy her. The Lord God watched carefully such suitors *and* enemies. He remembered his rivals, he marked her enemies, he noted *her* weaknesses and chronicled her every distraction and distracter.

Recalling a serpent that had once beguiled Eve, he vowed, *"That one* must go!" Recalling that a simple thing like bread had caused her to stumble in the wilderness, he affirmed within his being, "When there comes the daughter of this woman, that daughter shall not live by bread alone."

He saw the world and its glittery trinkets distract her, and he swore by himself, "That glitter, and its author, will I annihilate." But most of all, he observed the utter weakness and helplessness of her life in the face of any temptation and all sin. Once more he was provoked to declare, "Her daughter—my bride—shall live, by *another* and higher life!"

Chapter 19

Out of Egypt had come this girl. She crossed a searing wilderness, and in the land of promise she found rest and prosperity. But in her prosperity she moved farther and farther from her Lord.

Again and again he issued forth to her a cry:

Return to me.
Return to me!

But return she would not. Rather she went awhoring with the nations of the world.

Unnoticed by her, but well observed by her enemies, her wayward wandering from her God had caused her to lose the great strength he had bestowed upon her.

At last a brokenhearted God was forced to cry,

Do you not know I love you?
Yet though I love you
I must chasten you.
And when you wander from me,
there is no higher proof of my love
than this:

I will chastise you
and thereby bring you back to myself.

So she fell from weakness to weakness. A nation once abundant in strength and greatness became the vassal of even the weakest of nations.

Still she would not return to him.

"There is left to me, then, no other resource but one," sighed the Lord.

Chapter 20

He began to call forth prophets—men born in the South—to go into all the land to warn his people of coming judgment.

The prophets went forth, crying out again and again,

> *Repent!*
> *Repent!*
> *Turn back to the Lord,*
> *your lover.*

Some of these prophets journeyed to the North and cried out against the wantonness and godlessness of the people there.

To these prophets the people of the South listened only slightly; the North listened not at all.

There were no prophets from the North. There was, though, a young man from the North who fell in love with a most beautiful young girl in his village. He poured out upon her his whole affection, and soon they were married. But just as soon, she left him—to sell her body for the pleasures of sin. She made her abode in the world; and in its dregs and in her wickedness, she forgot the young man who had loved her so.

It was to the ears of this young man that there came, one awful day, the voice of the Lord.

> *Go, Hosea, go to your people.*
> *Cry out to them.*
> *Cry out with tongue,*
> *cry out with pen.*
> *Denounce their*
> *evil deeds.*
> *Call them to me.*
>
> *But before you go,*
> *search through this land.*
> *Find that woman*
> *of harlotry;*
> *bring her to your*
> *home.*
> *Make her, once more,*
> *your bride.*

Hosea clutched his ears at hearing these words. In revulsion he wept at the thought of touching again one so unclean. Nonetheless, he obeyed. From village to village he sought her. In dark and foul places he searched until at last he found her—found her in stupefying sin and filthy indifference.

Into his arms he lifted her, brought her into his home, and betrothed her again to himself.

"What have you done, Hosea?" came the voice of the Lord.

"Though she be a whore, I have taken her back," replied Hosea.

"So . . . I . . . the Lord God, will also receive again this whore, Israel. I will search her out in her sin; I will forgive her and bring her again into my house."

And together they sat down, and together they wept.

Chapter 21

When the cup was full and the time complete, the Lord allowed the North to be swept forever from the pages of history. And when grace had reached its ends, the Lord allowed the South to be conquered and the whole people led off in chains, across hot, dreary, and endless deserts, to another land.

Days turned to weeks as they traversed those burning sands. With each step they dragged their chains and thought of their forefathers in Egypt. At last they came to a city that once worshiped God but now worshiped bugs. A people whom God had once led out of slavery was led into slavery by that same Lord.

Chapter 22

Behold one, there, trudging along a hot dusty road in southern Babylon. For twenty-two years he has made his weary way from village to village, from city to city, comforting God's people, assuring them of eventual deliverance, and rebuking them for their sin. His shoulders are bent, his body stooped, for he carries in his soul the burden of his home, even the city of God, lying far away . . . still and desolate, a heap of ashes. His heart is filled, even at this moment, with sad and youthful memories of her destruction . . . and of a people who would not turn again to their Lord.

As the old man fought his way against hot winds and blowing sands of this Chaldean wasteland, his solitary thoughts were invaded by a small, shrill cry. The old prophet whirled about to discover the source of so tiny and so pitiable a call. Running to the side of the road, he furiously pulled back the dried bushes, there to discover, lying in the ditch, a newborn babe. Its body was wrapped in the sack of afterbirth, its cord uncut. The child was gasping its last, small breath.

The old prophet ripped open the sack and

breathed into the infant's lungs. Clutching the filthy child to his bosom, he ran toward the nearest house.

Late that evening the weary old man bade good night to a childless family among his own people who had taken the infant. As he slipped out onto the dusty road once more, his mind remained transfixed on the tragic state of the child whose life he had saved. A stirring was beginning to evidence itself deep in his heart when he heard a voice from behind him.

Ezekiel!

The old prophet stopped. He dared not move nor even breathe, for he knew too well *that* voice. And its coming did not always bode well for him.

Ezekiel!

"Yes, my Lord," he replied to open skies.

"The child . . . the one you found in the ditch."

"Yes, Lord."

"Ezekiel, as you did, I once walked down a desolate road. I, too, heard the cry of a tiny infant. It, too, was wrapped in its mother's afterbirth, and it, too, was dying. The mother of that dying babe was a Hittite, unclean. Its father, an Amorite, unclean! The child was an ugly, unloved, unlovable, filthy outcast . . . born of uncleanliness.

"I grasped that child to my bosom. I brought it to my home; there I washed the child, rubbed it with salt, nurtured and cared for it.

"The child was a girl. I gave her a name, *Jeru*. And because *I* raised her, she grew to be strong and beautiful. She was among the most beautiful of all women. In the days of Solomon she had become the most beautiful woman upon the face of the earth."

There was a long, dreadful pause. Ezekiel shuddered.

"On the day I would have taken her for my bride— on *that* day she heard the call of Egypt and Babylon. To them she gave up her virginity and her purity. She turned from me, walked the ways of the world, gave herself to fallen love. She became a harlot to Egypt and a slave in Babylon.

"Her gold they took from her; her silver, too. In the place of freedom, bondage. Instead of beauty, wrinkles. Her loveliness earned her only ruin. Yet, even now— though enslaved—Jeru will not return to me.

"Ezekiel, do you know of what I speak?"

Ezekiel turned his worn old face to the heavens, clamped his eyes closed, and in tight, measured words, responded. "Oh, my God, I know. I know!"

"For *me*, Ezekiel, go to that woman. Prophesy to her. Tell her to return to me. I will give her salve for her sores, clean garments for her rags. I will restore to her the beauty of her youth if she will but turn again to me."

There was another pause. Ezekiel's face turned again, his heart ached within his breast as he awaited once more the voice of the Lord. When it came, it came with such pathos that Ezekiel clutched his hands to his

ears, trying to hold back the sound of the agonizing of
God.

> *Return to me, Jeru.*
> *Return to your Creator.*
>
> *I have asked nothing*
> *save this,*
> *that you love me.*
>
> *With your mind,*
> *your heart,*
> *your soul,*
> *love me!*
>
> *Jeru, Jeru,*
> *return to me.*
> *Turn from your harlotry.*
> *Turn back,*
> *O city,*
> *turn back.*
> *Turn back, O bride of God.*
>
> *Return to me,*
> *O Jerusalem!*

Chapter 23

As the years rolled on, the story of the wayward nation changed but little. The beautiful woman strayed . . . returned . . . and strayed again. Each time she strayed, the Lord marked well those things that enticed her from him.

Patiently he watched the centuries come and go, waiting for the time he would step through the Door that separated time from eternity and there, on the stage of human drama, play out the role of the central figure of history.

And when he had marked every weakness and every enemy, he whispered, "The fullness of time is come. I am through with images, foreshadowings, symbols, and pictures! Now shall come reality. Now *I* shall have my counterpart."

He stepped from his throne and whispered to himself, "There is a village in Galilee." He raised his hand and called to one of the archangels.

Gabriel!

Chapter 24

To that enigmatic place, the portal between the physical and spiritual realms, he came. He had approached this Door many times before, had stepped out of the spiritual realm and plunged into the physical world, there to visit briefly for the purpose of some declaration, to alter history's spastic course, or to speak face to face with one of his prophets.

Today though, angels noted, something was different. As he stood before the open Door, rage burned upon his face; his eyes glowed white-hot. In all their long acquaintance with him they had never beheld such anger. Suddenly, a cry of terror ascended from the angels.

The Lord God *had disappeared.*

No more than an instant passed before they *knew* what he had done. And still amazement grew.

Often they had wondered why there remained but one who had no mate. Yet surely he would take no bride from angels nor fallen man. Nor could he—against his own word—create again.

He was a God of mystery, and somehow they *knew* his vanishing had something to do with a counterpart.

In that moment of consternation, Gabriel lifted his hand and announced:

Universal history is about to know
its greatest hour.
The Lord God is about to
incarnate himself
in the womb
of woman
and come forth
in the form
of human flesh.

Silence reigned for a moment. Grasping Gabriel's words and their meaning was beyond the bounds of angelic understanding.

What was it, there inside their God, that would drive him to such ends? God . . . in a likeness of fallen human flesh? A human in the form of a roach was more plausible.

Why? was their unspoken query.

"A counterpart," was their agreement.

"How?" was their unanimous question.

"We do not know," was their final conclusion.

His bride from the fallen human race, like Hosea's? Is it possible? The Holy God? Perhaps he will somehow seek to redeem her; but nothing that fallen could ever be *that* redeemed.

And yet, there it was: If he truly were to be born of a woman he would be God . . . visible. And if he were to become one of earth's inhabitants, he would be living in the realm where *all* species have a counterpart.

Obviously, there was something he knew that they did not know, a dimension of truth sealed off from their understanding.

This dimension of angelic ignorance became even more evident when they discovered he had chosen for his place of earthly birth not a castle, but a barn.

PART 3

Chapter 25

The little boy thrust his head through the partially open door and stared at the perspiring young man busy mending a piece of broken furniture.

"Have you heard the desert prophet?" inquired the little boy.

"No," came the genial reply of the young carpenter. "I have been quite occupied here of late. I am working alone now, as you know."

"Yes, and we all miss Joseph very much," came the little boy's quiet and sad response. "But anyway, I'm going to hear the desert prophet. Will you?"

"Yes," replied the carpenter, laying aside his finished work. "It is time I visited this prophet causing such a stir out there."

"Perhaps I will meet you there," replied the little boy. The door began to close, then opened again suddenly. The little boy's head reappeared.

"Is he not your brother, or something?"

"He is my cousin," came the reply.

"Ohhh, you must be very proud!" was the awed response.

"Very," replied the carpenter. "Very, very proud."

The door closed. The young carpenter looked about the room slowly, then—hesitantly—stored his mallet, his chisel, his tools of carpentry. Placing both hands upon the work table, he leaned forward and lowered his head.

"I have always been filled with the fires of the love of a God not old, and now to this has been joined the passion of the love of a young man. That love, dear earth, drives me to your salvation."

For a brief moment the carpenter closed his eyes; then, drawing into himself an unknown strength from some distant realm, he raised himself to his full stature and stepped out into the dusty street. With a gesture of finality he closed the door of his shop, turned, and spoke aloud.

"Well, brother John, it is time we met. I believe there is someone you wish to introduce to me."

Chapter 26

The desert floor was a furnace, the sun blinding in its brightness. Nonetheless, as far as the eye could see there were people. Some were standing, eyes closed. A few knelt. Many were weeping. Yet others, motionless, watched spellbound. All seemed oblivious to the scorching heat, their attention riveted on the fierce young prophet who stood upon a large rock in their midst. His voice rang like a silver trumpet, and as he spoke he turned, so that the fire of his gaze caught every eye.

For one brief moment his voice hesitated. It was something he thought he had seen at the edge of the crowd. Then, sure he had only imagined what he had so long hoped for, he continued. But there it was again—a light, too far back in the crowd for its source to be distinguished, but a light of unnatural origin. The desert prophet fell silent. He knew he was seeing what no other eye could see. He was seeing that for which he had been told to watch.

The light moved. It was coming toward the rocky mound. Something—or someone—was out there, and upon that one the glory of God was resting.

The crowd grew uneasy and began turning in the direction of John's stare. For just an instant the man—whoever he was—broke into a small open space. Spontaneously John roared,

Behold!

Every eye now turned. Again the young man came into view, and shock swept across the face of the Baptizer.

What is this
that God has done!
My childhood friend,
my next of kin,
'tis Mary's son!

Now, eagerly and purposefully, John verily thundered.

Behold,
the Lamb of God!

The two men reached toward one another and embraced, but even as they did, the young carpenter kept them moving in the direction of the river.

"Come, brother John, today we have something here to fulfill."

"And what might that be?" asked John.

"All righteousness," replied the carpenter, stepping into the water's depths.

Chapter 27

"Who was that man?" came a voice far out in the crowd.

"John, your words were strange. Are you not the Messiah?" came yet another inquiry.

Just in front of him stood two of his most zealous young disciples, their eyes still trying to keep in sight the young man who had so quickly disappeared beyond the crowd.

"John, please explain what just occurred," asked one of them, softly.

"No! I am *not* the Messiah!" rejoined the Baptizer. "Who, then, am I? I am the friend of the groom! I am come to introduce the groom—" He paused in mid-sentence, his right arm sweeping from one end of the throng to the other . . . "—to *his bride!*"

On hearing *this*, the two young men—who had thought they would be disciples of John until they drew their last breath—spontaneously turned and plunged into the crowd to follow the young Nazarene. They did not know this marked the first time since the Garden of Eden that man was seeking out God—to speak to him, unafraid, face to face.

Chapter 28

The Spirit within him drove him out into the wasteland, past all villages, all nomads, all water, out to where blazing sun and burning sand drained away his strength.

"It is here she was tempted," he whispered as he cast his eyes across the endless dunes of sand.

"She lived with me, *here*. I provided her every need, yet she would have forsaken me for bread. She tried me . . . once and again she tempted me, even dared me. She preferred to worship a calf of gold than to deal with the greater task of worshiping a God she could not see."

He would have raised himself to a higher vantage point, but forty days without nourishment had taken a dreadful toll upon his body. The young carpenter collapsed and fell into the searing sand.

A few minutes later he woke with a start and struggled to his feet.

"There is someone here. Nearby! How could anyone find this forsaken place?"

In the distance he saw a beautiful, shimmering

light—a light very definitely moving *toward* him, gliding smoothly over boulder and sand . . . as a serpent might glide across the earth.

"'Tis he!" cried the carpenter as he balanced himself and then ran, unhesitatingly, toward the glowing figure. The distance separating them diminished quickly as they approached one another. Suddenly, both paused. Like two gladiators they circled, each eyeing the other in wonder.

So this is the one who came to my ancestor, Adam! thought the carpenter as he searched out every feature of the beautiful creature before him.

"So this is God . . . in human form!" cried the other to himself, hardly able to hide his bitter joy! "God, visible! God, locatable! God, here, in dimension, space, and time! God, on *my* planet! God, incarnate inside the flimsy protection of blood, bone, and skin! God, *vulnerable!*

"God—*killable!*" he almost cried aloud.

Never had the adversary dared dream of such a dark and wondrous opportunity!

The fallen archangel at last broke the silence. His voice was enchanting, containing all the loveliness of the spheres.

"Sooo," he sang. "So, the one claiming to be the Son of God."

"I am Jesus of Nazareth. A carpenter by trade. Born of woman."

"Are you not the Son of God?" demanded the

shimmering creature. With those words—and that challenge—the angel of light reached down and cradled a large, smooth stone in his hand.

"You are hungry! Weak unto *death*," he continued, biting out the last word. "If you are the Son of God, here! Turn this stone to bread and *eat!*"

The young carpenter stared long at the stone.

So this is how it feels to be a man tempted—face to face—by the tempter. So this is how my creation, Adam, felt that day in the garden. Ah, and here I am now, receiving the same temptation Israel did when she was in the selfsame desert . . . lo, even in this very place!

As the young man stared at the stone, he felt the ache in his belly, the renewed spasms in his legs. Then, lifting his head and looking full face into the eyes of the waiting angel, he wavered. He was *feeling* temptation now, and he knew it. From deep within his bosom he began to recall the ancient times. Heard *his* own words! Strength surged out of his Spirit into his body!

"Lucifer! Have you forgotten? It is I who recorded it! '*Man* shall not live by bread alone.'

"*Man* shall *live!* He shall live. . . ." The carpenter moved his hand toward his own bosom. "Man shall live by *every* word that is spoken from the mouth of God!"

A moment of rage flickered across the face of the angel. Then, smiling gently, he raised his hand. Instantly the scene changed and the two were standing atop the highest pinnacle of the temple. The carpenter was poised precariously at its edge.

"If you are the Son of *God*, jump . . . from *here!* You know full well it is written that God will command *his* angels to guard you. *They* will not allow you to strike the stone below," he continued sweetly. "The angels will bear you up."

The carpenter eyed the dazzling heights. His weakened frame began to collapse under him. But in the same instant the unseen realm opened before him. It was true—he could see them—a legion of angels were poised to lunge forth at his slightest word.

Again his mind raced back to Israel. So often she had dared question his care for her. Again, his own words welled up from within his inmost being. His knees braced. Boldly, even serenely, he turned.

"Lucifer, have you forgotten? I have recorded it: 'You shall not tempt the Lord, *your* God.'"

The archangel, caught off guard by so sure a response, was dazed by the carpenter's words. For an instant his own knees, which in a bygone age had so often bent to his God, momentarily buckled. Quickly he jerked himself free of this brief sanity and raised his hand again.

Once more the scene changed.

They were now on some high mountain overlooking the whole world. Below them, glistening in garland beauty, were all the great kingdoms of the past; beside them the kingdoms of the present. Beyond them, plainly visible out there in the future, were kingdoms yet unknown. Some were glorious, some powerful, others sparkling in splendor.

"You have come, *I* know why," hissed the angel. "You have come to rule the land! To rule earth. Then let us make short work of your task. You know that all kingdoms upon earth—past, present, and future—are mine and mine alone. All governments are *mine!*" The angel paused, giving full opportunity for a rejoinder.

The carpenter chose not to challenge a statement both knew to be true. The angel moved very close, his words sounding like the chimes of heaven.

"I will give to you these kingdoms, *all* of them! You may rule them all—and this whole planet with them! They are not only mine, but I may *give* them . . . to whomever I please."

Again the carpenter disputed not the angel's words.

"I will give them all . . . to you. You need do but one thing, and one thing only: Fall down here . . . now . . . and worship *me!*"

The young man looked again at the kingdoms. Every fiber in his being ached. He was weary beyond words. Tired, terribly tired. The task before him seemed so wearisome, so unutterably difficult, with a price to be paid that seemed, for a moment, far too great.

But once more the young man bolted upright. Something he had said to Israel long ago began singing within his depths.

Be gone, Satan!
It has been recorded,
"You shall worship the Lord, your God!
You will serve him . . . him, alone!"

The angel quaked in astonishment at so strong a rejoinder. For an instant his body spasmed, his face contracted, the light of his being dimmed. Slowly he willed back his strength, the glow of his light brightening once more.

"I shall leave you . . . for the moment."

At the very instant the fallen archangel vanished, a company of elect angels appeared, even as their Lord crumpled upon the rocks.

After a few moments of angelic care, the perilously weak man opened his eyes. A smile broke across his blistered face; words formed upon his cracked lips.

Did you see?
I ask,
Did you see!

The angels nodded an embarrassed assent.

"Did you see!" he cried again, struggling to his feet. "I beat him! Neither was the garden scene nor Israel's fate repeated here, this day. It was a *man* who lost to Satan in the garden that day. This time Satan lost. And he lost to a *man!* He lost to me, not as God. He lost to me . . . as man! As surely as he once beguiled man, today he lost . . . to . . . a . . . *man!"*

The carpenter staggered toward a rock, while angels, quite unaccustomed to such unprecedented behavior, stepped back. The man from Nazareth braced himself against a boulder, raised his head toward a starry, moonlit sky, and cried aloud,

"I beat him. I, Jesus of Nazareth, beat him."

Now standing erect, he threw his head heavenward and cried again.

Soon—
Yes, soon now—
Very, very soon!

Chapter 29

"To a wedding?"

"Yes, I am going to a wedding in Cana," replied his mother. "They are friends of mine. They have asked that I also invite you."

"To a wedding . . ." He repeated the words, slowly. "Yes, it is a matter to consider; after all, I came to earth for a . . ." His words ended there, but his mother understood.

That evening at the appointed time, Mary departed for the wedding without her son, as he was deep in consultation with that small band of men who followed him.

Later that evening he made his way to the little village where his mother had earlier gone, pensively wandering its narrow streets, watching the people making their way home from a day's work, listening to the conversations coming from within the houses, observing the creaking carts coming back from the marketplace. Everyone, it seemed to him, appeared so tired, their countenances so very empty. Joy seemed to have departed this place. Everything, in *his* eyes, appeared so *old*.

His ears caught the sound of festivity. *The wedding. There will be joy enough there.* His pace quickened.

It was through a small entrance in the rear that the young carpenter entered the wedding hall, very late and quite unnoticed. He made his way to an obscure place far to the back of the crowded room and began observing the proceedings of the evening with unusual interest.

At the center of the festivities was a huge banquet table, laden with all manner of delightful foods. There was the groom, so young, and his bride, so beautiful. Both were obviously very much in love. And, truly, the room was filled with an atmosphere of joy.

Mary was speaking with the young couple. Just as she was about to turn away, he noticed that the groom was called aside by two very worried looking servants.

So this is how it is. Multitudes here. The beautiful bride, the bridegroom. The wine. Yes, so it will be when I . . .

His thoughts were intruded upon by some deeper scene *within* him. He looked again at the hall and the wedding guests. The divine eyes within him began looking past the crowded room, to some larger scene. There was a crowd, yes, but it was the whole host of fallen mankind. Faces were sad, voices tired, witnessing to what was in the heart. Oldness hung in the air. The young carpenter sighed deeply, growing sad at the melancholy sight his inner eye beheld.

A gentle and familiar voice seemed to be calling him back to his earthly surroundings. For an instant he found himself watching both scenes at once—one, a whole world, the other, a local wedding. So different, yet so alike.

"They are out of wine!" came a voice.

It was his mother.

"Yes, I know," he said, increased in sadness by the view of his double scene and her pronouncement, so correct in its assessment.

Mary was accustomed to these interludes when his spirit and mind met between two realms. She paused a moment and repeated softly, "They are out of wine."

He turned and looked at her, the vision of a sad world still lingering in his sight . . . a world so desperately in need of redemptive joy.

"Woman, do you know what you are asking of me? My time has not yet come!"

"I know," she whispered again, reassuringly. "Still, right now, *this* wedding is out of wine!" And with that she turned away, missing the soft smile that broke upon his face. Mary crossed the room to the groom and his two distraught servants. "I believe you are out of wine, are you not?"

"Yes, we are. And there is none to be found in all the village. We have searched everywhere. It seems the whole world is out of wine."

"I offer this suggestion, then," she replied. "Do

you see the young man over there, the one sitting in the farthest corner?"

The face of one of the servants grew ashen. "Oh, my . . . I did not know *he* was here. It is the carpenter turned prophet. Oh my!"

"Go to him. Whatever he tells you to do, do it!"

The two servants exchanged puzzled glances. One shrugged his shoulders, and with that the two men began moving cautiously across the hall.

"Uh, sir. We . . . we are out of wine."

"Yes, I know. You have been out of wine for a long, long time."

Once more the two men exchanged looks of consternation.

"Sir, what shall we do? There must be wine at the close; it is a custom."

"A good custom indeed," said the carpenter. "What you need is a new wine. The *best* wine, saved for the very *last!* Do you see those six large pots over there?"

"Yes, but sir, we cannot use those pots. They are for the rite of purification; they are for the dead."

"Go. Fill those pots with water. After that, take what comes from them to the director of the wedding. He will tell you what to do."

The servants stared. "Sir . . . ?"

"Go."

"Yes, sir."

As the servants turned, one murmured aloud,

"Pots of death. What does he expect to come out of the likes of them?"

For a long time the young carpenter continued to watch. His mind and heart were fertile with thoughts—thoughts similar, perhaps, to those of any young man on such an occasion, contemplating his own future wedding plans.

The festivities had obviously been drawing to a close, but now a new energy, a new delight, was making its way across the room. Something had sparked the revelry in everyone. And why not? After all, they now had 150 gallons of *delicious* new wine!

The Nazarene carpenter slipped from the crowded room, unnoticed, and once more stepped out into Cana's night. He paused for a moment, his attention drawn to a conversation taking place at the door of the banquet hall. It was the wedding director bidding good night to some of the guests.

"Never, in all my years," said he. "Never! Always before, the groom waits until the end and brings out the worst wine! In many a case, I tell you, no wine at all would have been better. But tonight—ah, tonight! At the very end—at the *end*, mind you—the groom brought out the best wine I have ever tasted here or anywhere. Wine," he laughed, "the likes of which has not been served since the dawn of creation.

"What an idea! The best wine, at the very end. What a *glorious* idea!"

Chapter 30

"What did he say to me when first I met him?" responded the Levite to his friend Jude, as the two men moved slowly along with the throng.

"I was sitting at a table collecting taxes. No, that is not exactly accurate. Actually, business was slow, as it often is with tax collectors, so I was using my time to memorize a list!"

"A list?" rejoined Jude.

"Yes. I have memorized dozens of them. Mostly laws. You know, do this, do not do this; this is a sin, this is not. This is right, that is wrong! You see, I *had* an ambition. Oh, what an ambition! To know every law of our religion. To know every rule there was to know and to keep them *all!*"

Matthew ended his words with a hearty laugh.

"Anyway, I was sitting there when along came a crowd of people . . . one very much like this one. Such a commotion, and I wondered for what. Then I saw. Ah, it was *he!* He walked over to where I sat, stared at me, or right through me, and then said:

Matthew, I will fulfill

your laws. I will destroy the rules.
Now come, follow me.

Matthew laughed again. "Now I keep a new list."

"You do?" said his surprised friend. "Of what?"

"I keep a list of all the things he has said he would fulfill, do away with, abolish, void, bring down, conclude, destroy, or annihilate! It grows, I might add, almost daily."

Jude smiled. "May I impose on you and ask to hear the contents of *this* list? Dare I call such a thing a list? It sounds more like the roll call of Judgment Day."

"Let us see," responded Matthew enthusiastically. "So far, of things marked for obliteration, I have the law, rules, Satan (if you please) and his angelic host, demons, governments, the world's system. Mind you this one: all realms seen and unseen. In fact, as best I can understand him, the . . . well, the entire cosmos. And then there are the Sabbath, holy days, rituals, the temple, observances, sin, creation, and . . ."

The two men stopped, as had the crowd around them. Something up ahead was now obstructing their path. Whatever it was, the young carpenter was taking an exceptional interest in it.

"See that look on his face, Matthew? Well, I have seen it before, on rare occasions. All memorable, I might add. And unless I miss a fair guess, you are going to be adding to that list of yours quite soon."

Chapter 31

Out of the city of Nain, moving toward a burial ground, came a moaning, wailing procession. At the first sight of it, the carpenter had come to a sudden stop. The beating drums, the cadence of the clattering sticks, and the cry of the professional wailer held him almost spellbound. Or perhaps it was not these at all that so firmly held his attention. Was it, rather, something he was viewing that no mortal eye could see?

There was a woman in the procession, a widow. Following behind her were four men. Upon their shoulders rested a bier, cradling the lifeless form of a young boy. But was there more?

Yes, there was something else, but only those who see the unseen could know of its presence. *He* could see, and what he saw provoked first his interest, then his highest rage.

Upon the bier, dark and dreadful, stood the angel of death, holding the little boy fast within his cold domain.

The carpenter raised his hand. Time stood still. The two—the carpenter and the death angel—now stood alone, in realms spiritual. The young Nazarene, almost mad with rage, moved quickly toward the dark angel.

"You!" cried Death, in stunned amazement.

The carpenter shook his head slowly, for it was a grotesque and hideous thing that was standing before him. He sighed, and thought within,

> *Can it be*
> *that I*
> *who made the lamb*
> *made thee?*

"We have met before," spoke the carpenter aloud, a hint of challenge in his voice.

"Yes," came the gurgling voice of Death. "You prevented me from my appointed task, and held from me my rightful prey that night. Ah, but here, today, you are too late, Son of God! See! This one is *already* mine. Even now my domain is his abode . . . and *none* can tread there. Nothing," roared the dark angel, "no power, no hope, no dream, no prayer can reach him now! This is not as it was when last we met in Egypt on the first night of Passover. . . . *This* time you have come too late!"

Death's cold glare was returned by eyes blazing with unmitigated rage. Rage so great that even Death shuddered at the sight of such unbridled fury.

"You know not all things, immortal Death," replied the young carpenter, as he spoke through clenched teeth.

The young man raised his hand again. Time's scene reappeared. Quickly the carpenter walked to the middle of the road; the funeral processional came to an abrupt halt. The four men, a little uncertain of what was happening, lowered the bier to the ground. A crowd of people, and all their thoughts, stood still at the sight of a man so utterly consumed with livid rage.

The carpenter knelt beside the child, reaching out his hand to touch him. A cry went up from the child's mother. "Lord, touch him not, for it is written we are not to touch the uncleanness of death."

The young man raised his head, narrowed his eyes upon the dark angel, and replied, "Death? What death?"

The death angel sneered, bent low, and tightened his grip upon the child.

Ever so gently the kneeling carpenter continued moving his hand toward the boy. As the carpenter's hand reached, not the child, but the hand of Death, the dark angel screamed in astonishment, tearing his hand away in frothing agony. The crowd broke out in wild cries of fear and joy. The young boy opened his eyes and sat up.

While chaotic ecstasy reigned over the crowd, the young carpenter moved swiftly down the road to intercept again that black and terrible creature who bore the name Azell.

"Halt!" thundered the Lord as he stepped past time and entered again the unseen realms.

For the first time since he had been loosed upon creation that awful day in the garden, the angel of death obeyed the command of another.

"Death! Damned Death," cried the Lord, now at the very edge of self-control. "Hear me, Death! Damned . . . doomed . . . Death! Ere my bride appears upon the scene . . . you, Azell . . . you, Death . . . *you* shall die!"

The young carpenter turned away. Upon his face, where rage had burned in full fury but a moment before, there was now the serene glow of triumph.

"Matthew."

"Yes, I know, Jude," replied the Levite, fumbling through the pockets of his cloak. "Now where *did* I put that list?"

Chapter 32

The carpenter was very tired; the day had been long and trouble-filled. If he did not hurry, he would be late for a banquet being given in his honor, but the crowd pressed in against him from all sides. Movement in this melee was difficult at best.

Above the din that rose around him came another sound—one not natural to this realm.

It came again—a long, mournful wail. All other voices fell silent, all eyes searched for the source of this eerie chant. A song out of hell it was, piercing the bravest soul with icy fear. Children ran away, some people covered their ears, while others drew their garments tightly about them.

The young carpenter responded instantly, forcing his way through a human sea toward the ghastly cry. His very demeanor caused a path in the crowd to open before him, revealing at its edge a strange creature from whom rose the fiendish music.

Suddenly her wailing stopped. In its place came hard, labored breathing interspersed with snarls and whines. Her long hair hung so tangled about her head and shoulders it was not clear which direction she faced.

Then, from beneath that matted mess, she thrust forth two defiant hands, clawlike, with which she jerked back her hair, revealing a blurred and twisted face. A sick groan went up from the crowd. Her face was filthy, her eyes glazed. She turned toward the sun, searching its fire as one attempting to find a way back to reality.

The carpenter stepped in her path, his shadow falling upon her face. She whimpered, then struggled, obviously trying again—vainly—to pull herself free of something . . . to understand . . . anything.

Her glazed eyes met his. She twisted for a brief instant, then a hideous, wicked smile grew upon her face. The wail began again—this time higher, more obscene than before. Her dark music would drop, then rise again, a demonic psalm celebrating some perverse triumph. Its wretched cadence was somehow flaunting that triumph at the young Nazarene.

The carpenter knew the meaning of the wail. He knew its source, and he knew it was the bondage which held this girl that was being so gleefully trumpeted.

Who was this girl?

The very daughter of Israel—the offspring of a whore.

As her mother had been, so was she. Her mother had gone into sin with Egypt and Babylon; so also had the daughter followed willingly in her mother's steps.

While only a child, this one had been willful, head-strong, and rebellious. When she discovered that men lusted after her body, she was both intoxicated with a sense of power and filled with bitter contempt toward her suitors. She gave her body at first, but as she grew older and wiser, she placed a price upon it. Contempt grew deeper, rebellion more violent, yet she gloried in her sin and wore with pride the title of harlot. Little by little the dark forces of the netherworld made home in her fleshly being.

"Truly, the daughter of Jeru," sighed the Galilean.

The wail subsided; again the girl struggled against some unseen force. Then came a sneer, followed by a laugh—a defiant, derisive laugh, aimed straight at the prophet from Galilee.

Every eye that watched seemed to understand that something—or someone—within her was making sport of the young prophet, though the point of the taunt was unclear.

Pity, anger, and understanding welled up from within the Nazarene. But more. Springing first from his heart, then surging across his face, was the unmistakable look of love!

What was it about this prostitute that so captured the Lord's attention?

A high moment in divine history was about to unfold.

The carpenter searched the young girl's face. He looked past the wild, hollow eyes. He saw the loneliness, the pain, the scars, the aged look upon one so young. He saw the hurt, the sense of betrayal; he saw the frantic terror that even now gripped her heart, and heard again the muted cry for help.

He looked past the outward horror, the cynicism, the cuts, the snarls and growls, the heinous laughter. He saw the demon in her—no, seven demons. He saw the soul, dark, in need of redemption. But deeper still penetrated his divine gaze! He saw the human spirit—a lifeless, gray thing. The human spirit—an element found in the bosom of every human being, yet belonging to the heavenly realm—lying there, cold and dead since the days of fallen Adam.

Looking yet deeper, he saw something else. A beautiful, beautiful young girl. But was this possible?

He raised his hand.

The young carpenter no longer saw the girl or the crowd around them. He was looking back into eternity, even to the age before the eternals, to a moment known to no other—that moment when he had marked off portions of his own divine nature . . . had marked them off that they might one day be portions of . . .

He saw it! A portion of his being that had been the *very first* to be marked off.

He dropped his hand. He looked again at that dead spirit within the girl.

*Her spirit is **destined**
to be made alive—**again!***

Marked off in me,
before the foundation of the age.
Determined, even then,
*that **this one** would become . . .*

Something in the young girl sensed the intensity of his searching gaze. Falling back, the girl began to howl and snap. Her rage and cursing spiraled into madness.

The carpenter responded instantly. Thrusting out his hand, he pointed directly at the girl. In an earthshaking voice that reverberated like a thunderclap, he cried,

*She is **not** yours!*
Leave her.
Come out!
Now and forever.

The young girl's body contorted, her eyes filled with terror. She clutched her head as in some indescribable pain. The obscene wail lifted from her. The girl let out a soul-freezing scream and crumpled to the ground. There was no doubt in anyone's mind. The girl was dead.

Instinctively, several women rushed to where the young girl's lifeless body had fallen. They pulled back her hair and stared in dumbfounded amazement.

The girl was asleep, a faint hint of tranquil peace upon her face.

And while no one was noticing, the young carpen-

ter stole away, almost tardy now for a dinner engage-
ment.

And the girl, left lying there on the ground . . . who
is she?

Who, *really*, is this girl?

Chapter 33

The wealthiest man in the city, and a Pharisee—rich and religious. Such would be the carpenter's host this evening.

He was greeted at the door of the luxurious mansion by a well-dressed servant who quickly ushered him through the home and out into a large, open garden. Not far away, on the city wall, the outline of the watchman's turret could be seen under a moonlit sky.

Spread out on the ground at the center of the garden was a vast tapestry covered with an endless array of exotic foods. Everywhere, it seemed, servants were scurrying about, some leading guests to their appointed place, others bringing more huge trays of delicacies into the garden.

Among the guests present were the leading citizens of the city.

Simon, standing at the rear of the garden, motioned for the young prophet to come and take the *second* highest place of honor in the banquet room. The host then rang a small bell. Following their host's example, everyone knelt and then reclined and started eating.

There was music, wine, laughter, and an atmosphere of relaxed revelry. All evidence pointed to a delightful evening with a wealthy host and a famous young prophet. Perhaps there might even be a time for addressing questions to the honored guest. But such would not be the turn of things.

Only a few minutes into the meal there was a commotion at the door, enough to catch the attention of a few eyes, which in turn provoked a flurry of whispers. In a moment the garden was dead silent. Standing in the doorway was a woman of the street. The loudest sound now was the strained breathing of a hundred souls. From somewhere came the words,

It is a whore!

Simon was mortified. Such an intrusion, by a woman of the street, here . . . in *his* home. With *this* guest present. Unbelievable.

For a long moment, the young girl stood motionless in the doorway. All knew her, and some marveled that she was neither afraid nor ashamed. She seemed, rather, almost serene.

They wondered when that shrill, unearthly wail would commence, but some observed that she seemed changed in every way.

The Galilean guest, in the meantime, continued eating, not even bothering to look up.

The young girl began moving. The electric tension in the room soared, for there was no doubt as to her destination. Every eye watched, transfixed, as the young girl moved across the garden and took her place just behind the young prophet, even at his feet.

Turning to look over his shoulder, the young man acknowledged the girl's presence for the first time. For an incredibly long moment nothing in the room moved.

Then the girl pulled from her cloak a beautiful vase, obviously filled with some exotic and terribly expensive oil, its contents undoubtedly representing her whole life's possessions. With uncommon grace and a dignity bordering on regality, she broke open one end of the vase and slipped to her knees. The garden was immediately filled with a rich, intoxicating scent of exotic perfume.

Simon stared, horrified, trying not to believe that an unclean woman was such a short distance from him *and* at the very feet of the young prophet. He turned to one of the dignitaries and said in a whisper that was meant to be heard, "Surely, if this man is a prophet, he knows she is a street woman, defiled! Surely he will not allow her to touch him."

Yet others whispered loudly, "Surely she will not touch *him*. He is a man of God!" The young girl began to pour the precious oil upon the feet of the carpenter. As she did, she lifted first her face, and then a hand, heavenward, while hot tears poured softly down her face. Soon the tears were falling upon his feet, mingling with the oil.

The carpenter made no protest, nor did he stir.

A murmur of shocked disbelief filled the room as the woman of sin began to bathe his feet with oil and tears. Reaching down, she lovingly—even passionately—began kissing his feet.

And from the city walls the watchman of the night called out the evening psalm:

*Thou shalt
love the Lord
thy God
with all thy soul,
and all thy heart,
and all thy might.*

But *no one* seemed to have heard. And those who heard did not understand.

Now, taking the tresses of her long and beautiful hair, the young girl wrapped them tightly together, forming them into a towel, and began to wipe his feet. She wiped them dry—except for her newest tears.

Who, pray tell, is this incredible young girl?

Chapter 34

"Simon."

The young prophet broke his silence in a quiet, disconcertingly calm voice.

"Simon, you are a man who cares for the things of God. You have given this banquet in my honor, have you not?"

"Yes, that is true."

"When I came into your home, Simon, there was no kiss of greeting upon my cheek; no servant washed from my feet the dirt of this day. But this woman whom you have called a woman of sin has come and washed my feet, not with water, but with the costliest of oils . . . and with her tears. Further, she has kissed them dry with her lips.

"Now, Simon, I have a question for you. Two men owed great debts to a king, but one owed a greater sum. The king forgave them both their debts. Which one, Simon, do you suppose loved the king the more?"

Simon had turned a bright crimson in anger and embarrassment. He bit off every word of his reply.

"Well, Lord, the one who owed the greater debt, I suppose."

"You have spoken the truth, Simon."

The young prophet stood and, as he did, he faced the girl. He reached out his hand, and lifted her to her feet.

"Truly, the one forgiven little, loves little. The one forgiven much, loves much." He stared straight at the young girl . . . whose face had become a river of sparkling tears.

"You are forgiven and cleansed. All is past, as though it never had been."

The young girl looked at him as though she understood the furthest depths of his every word.

"Now, child, go . . . and sin no more."

The young girl did not move. Rather, she dropped, once more, to her knees.

"My Lord, and my God. I am cleansed . . . and I shall sin no more. But I shall never . . . never . . . go away."

Chapter 35

About twenty men and four women accompanied him wherever he traveled. From the day of her deliverance, she did not ask, she simply *became* part of that little band of followers. Wherever he went, she went, and poured out her whole love and her whole life on him.

In the earliest hours of the morning she could be found preparing his breakfast. When he sat down to teach, *she* was there, at his feet. When he departed, she departed with him. When those twenty men asked too much of him, she quietly, firmly, protested. She washed his feet, served his meals, cared for his clothes, placed fruit beside his bed in the evenings. He who said of himself, "I am the living water," always had cool water to drink—brought by *her* hands. When nights were cold, she made sure the house where he was guested would be warm. In the hot, blistering sun of summer, she walked with the little band of followers, village to village, city to city—always following *him*.

Why such devotion?

Because she adored him. Fervently, single-mindedly, she loved him. She was totally enamored, completely enraptured, and utterly in love with her Lord and Master. She did not care who knew it. She was embarrassingly unembarrassed about the matter.

The others eventually grew used to the sight of her single-minded adoration and her uninhibited outpouring of affection, which continued unceasingly from earliest dawn to the last light of night.

They even learned from her. Oh, they *all* professed a love for him that was equal to hers. But they *spoke* of overthrowing Rome, of abolishing the present Hebrew state, of setting up a spectacular throne, of avenging the vicious rumors that seemed always to be spread about concerning their Lord. They dreamed of wielding both political and spiritual power, of casting out demons, of throwing Caesar into a dungeon and Satan into a burning pit.

They professed love, but talked power and fame. Little by little they changed. As months turned to years, they spoke less of conquest and got down to the business of loving their God.

The most amazing thing of all was this: He responded. He poured out love in return. It seemed a little odd, the Son of God, caring, affectionate, loving, and returning love . . . so profoundly, so totally. That God might love, with such ardor, was simply something that had never occurred to them. Nor could they quite understand why they found it so difficult to express love toward him.

Her mother before her had failed at this same

simple matter for centuries, but now, before all eyes, this simple girl was unfolding the highest order of the universe. To *love* her God.

Watching her, they learned. For though she expressed her love in service and care, she expressed her love yet more in eyes, in heart, in soul, and in the fervor and passion of her whole being. No abstraction, this love. An unnerving thing this. Unwavering, day after day, with total abandon—loving him. You saw it in her eyes, in her kneeling, in moments of praise and rejoicing, and when she looked into his face—which was almost always.

Who is this girl . . . this *incredible* girl?

Chapter 36

That ancient sense of aloneness had gripped him once more. Slipping away from everyone, he left the city and slowly made his way up the slopes of the Mount of Olives. At a good vantage point he stopped, knelt, and leaned back on one of the trees, there to view the city across the valley before him.

He had watched this city for over two thousand years; and for as many years she had broken his heart. He sighed, pressed his chin into his hands, and began to weep.

His gaze intensified, and the sight of the city below gave way to a divine sight. Slowly the city of people, houses, and temple drew together as one. Out from this swirling mosaic began to emerge a single form. In the place of the city there appeared, standing in the valley across from him, a young and very beautiful woman. She was robed all in white.

He uttered but one word,

Jeru.

She was very young, and utterly beautiful. As he

looked at her, he recalled how she had come into this, the land of promise, and how she had made her home in the heartland of Judea. In those days her beauty and her innocence were breathtaking. Nonetheless, from the outset, she seemed to show an inordinate curiosity toward the strange ways of the people and gods of the surrounding lands. In the days of Solomon, at the zenith of her beauty, she broke her vows of betrothal with him and flung herself into *their* world.

For a long time he gazed at the girl, and as the minutes passed the young girl seemed to grow older. Her features hardened, as did her heart.

He knew. Soon she would join with others in killing the very One to whom she had been betrothed. But more. He knew very soon that Jeru would also *die!* Die, never to rise again.

Not only she, but all those who had enticed her from him.

My rivals, my enemies—all will soon come to an end. In her place will arise a spiritual being of whom you, Jeru, have been but a picture. Another will come, far more beautiful than you. A new—

But his thoughts were abruptly interrupted.

"My Lord, I would not have disturbed you, but it is important—very important."

"Yes?"

"We have wind of a plot. Of the details we are uncertain, but it appears someone . . ."

"Yes, I know. I have known for a long, long time.

Do not concern yourself. It is a matter being carefully watched by my Father. Now, may I ask a favor? Would you wait for me at the base of the mount? I would be alone for a moment longer."

"Yes, Lord," responded the disciple, turning to make a hasty retreat from the hill's summit.

Again he turned his eye back to the city below. The awful realization of what this ancient city really was engulfed him again. Through gushing tears and sobs of sorrow, he cried out.

"O Jerusalem, Jerusalem. You have so often stoned the very ones who came to save you. How often have they called you . . . have *I* called you . . . to return. But you would not. How oft would I have taken you in my arms as a hen does her brood, but you would not."

O, Jeru,
Jeru, Jerusalem,
Tonight, seal your fate . . . forever.

Chapter 37

Later that night a lonely figure was led from his place of prayer in an olive grove to the hall of judgment, there to be tried for blasphemy against God. A few had loved him, but many more had hated him.

The midnight trial made that fact evident. His words were twisted; false witnesses reported to the city fathers the words that had to be said. The point in it all was obvious. They did not want this troublesome Galilean to exist any longer.

"This one is not worthy of life." That was the final verdict. He was led from the hall to his appointment with death.

Strange, is it not, what sometimes crosses the mind of a man facing death. He was recalling a moment in the distant past. A conversation.

"Adam, do you see this seed? Within me, and within this seed, is a principle that cannot be rescinded. If the seed lives . . . it abides *alone*. But if the seed falls into the ground and dies . . .

"Sleep here, Adam. Or abide alone forever! *Live*, in aloneness. *Die*, and become many."

His thoughts were interrupted. It seems there had been a slight oversight. He would have to be tried again.

Chapter 38

Enemy occupation of the land necessitated a trial by the foreign government. The government of the Hebrews *and* the heathen government would have to be in agreement to end this man. Jew and Gentile must be one in this matter. And so they led him to Pilate's palace.

The carpenter observed carefully the face of the man who would try to rescue from execution an innocent victim who did not choose to be rescued.

The conversation between them touched on many things, including government.

"Before this day ends," the carpenter told him matter-of-factly, "*both* your governments, and *both* your races, will be executed with me. Hebrews and heathen will cease to exist."

With that comment, Pilate ordered the young prophet returned to his enemies.

Earthly governments had now agreed: He must die. But one more vote was needed for total unanimity. And so the citizens of the city were brought together to express their verdict.

The Galilean was led onto a balcony overlooking a

vast courtyard. The citizens of Jerusalem were there, as far as eye could see, shouting and screaming. His eyes blurred; the crowd before him began to spin in his vision. Slowly the scene reformed.

Before him stood his betrothed, Jeru. She raised her fist and shook it at him. Contempt and rage glowering in her face, she cried out her sentiments. "Away with him! Crucify him. Crucify him!" she demanded.

He turned his head and shut his eyes, trying to blot out the sight of hate so absolute. But she would make her choice clear. She cried again, "Crucify him! Crucify him!"

From deep within his being he groaned,

O, Jeru, Jeru—Jerusalem!

The verdict complete, the soldiers of heathendom now led their victim out of the court, into the street, and to an awaiting prison. Through dark chambers they led him, stripped him, and beat him . . . mercilessly.

For a moment he lost consciousness. When he awoke, he—as earth's first man once had done—instinctively reached for his side.

"No. Not yet. I am still whole."

He rolled over on the cold stone floor, tried to rise, but collapsed from pain. Between swollen lips he whispered,

Not yet, Adam. Not yet. But soon.

Chapter 39

Half blind, near death, he dragged the wooden beam up the loathsome hill. When he stumbled, a passerby was conscripted to complete the task.

Through blood-filled eyes he caught his first glimpse of Golgotha and heard the sound of hammers finishing their instrument of execution.

The soldiers turned the carpenter around so he might see what lay upon the ground before him.

The cross!

He had not seen it since *that* day . . . the day before the birth of eternity.

"The greatest instrument of destruction in the universe!" he whispered. He raised his bruised head and groped—with eyes nearly blind—to see if all else was in place. Yes, there the nails, the mallet, the derisive sign, the gall. All were present, having been inseparably linked to him for unnumbered ages.

Again he cast his eyes down at the cross lying before him. None on earth nor in the skies could e'er have guessed that beam of wood constituted the force that would annihilate the whole of creation.

But something was missing!

Slowly he looked about, surveying the whole macabre panorama. There it was! In the hands of a Roman soldier. The spear that would open his side.

Something within him, a sense of completion, filled his being. A soft smile struggled to the surface of his swollen face.

"On with it. Crucify him!" someone in the crowd screamed.

"Oh, you have no idea what shall be crucified this day," he murmured. Then, turning his eyes heavenward, he whispered again, addressing universes unseen, "All things are ready."

With that simple word the whole habitation of heavenly places emptied, as the angelic host hurled itself into time, there to fill every roof, hill, and mountain in and around Jerusalem. Ten thousand times ten thousand swords were drawn by outraged and weeping angels. Every sinew in them strained, waiting for a command—any command—that would allow them to unleash vengeance upon that hill.

Pitilessly the soldiers began to shove him down upon the beam of wood, only to discover his utter willingness to lie down upon this cross and stretch out his hands and feet. Nor did it escape their eyes that their captive opened his palms to the waiting nails.

One of the soldiers, hesitating for only a moment as he contemplated this strange man before him, reached for one of the long, cold spikes and the heavy iron mallet. He pressed the nail hard against the wrist and raised his hammer high into the air.

The carpenter raised his other hand slightly, and *space and time stood still!*

Within the very core of the spirits of every angel, bursting like fire, came the unspoken, and quite unbelievable, command of their Lord. For a single instant they hesitated.

"Now!" commanded the carpenter, "*All* things to the cross!"

Chapter 40

The young carpenter had given the angels not only a command but an ability. They could do something that, until now, only *he* had ever done. To accomplish his will he had now allowed his angels to become masters of space and time. They would know what only *I AM* had ever known before: for the next few moments they would be able to move to any point in time, space . . . or eternity. They could roam the corridors of universal time, breaking into any place in history. They could travel across all points of time—and to *many* places in eternity—moving, if necessary, in *both* directions of eternity, even to the age before the ages and, if need be, to the final end of all ages.

Hurtling faster than even they could conceive, each went to his appointed place to perform his Master's will.

Chapter 41

It was the angel who bore the simple name Messenger who plunged backward through all time, then back through all eternity past—even to that age before *all* things, *save God!* There, in eternity past, he found a lamb—slain—upon a wooden cross. Lifting high this trophy of endless love—a trophy, a death, a crucifixion unknown until now—he bore the slain lamb forward through eternity into time, and finally to Golgotha, there to make that cross—and lamb—one with the cursed tree and the carpenter who lay outstretched upon it. All points of time past and time future, all points of eternity past and eternity future, converged on that cross. A cross, and its crucified victim, slain before creation, had finally found its place in the continuum of time. And all things that had been crucified before the foundation of the world journeyed to Golgotha—from out of the past and from out of the future—to be crucified in *time!*

Yet another angel went to that long-forgotten place where Eve and Seth had once laid the body of an ancient Adam. The angel clutched into his arms the first-born of our race, and bore him forward through time, coming at last to Calvary.

Within the very bosom of Adam lay all the descendants of the human race, for they were—after all—*in* him. Further, in the bosom of that first man lay not only all mankind but also the Adamic fall, the curse, and the self-nature that had invaded, plundered, and twisted man's soul.

Adam, and all mankind *in* him, was carried in angelic hands to the place of the carpenter's execution, and there became one with the cross. Adam's race was crucified!

One of the archangels rose from earth's plane, stood above this planet, and called to time past and time future, commanding all governments, rules, dominions, and principalities from all earth's ages to come forth. Capturing them all in his mighty arms, he swept back into time's sphere and made flight toward Jerusalem. Standing before the cross, he waited . . . waited to see princes and principalities crucified upon the cross of our Lord!

But one of the angels did not stir from his place. Golgotha itself was his appointment. On one side of the cross stood a crowd of Hebrews. On the other side, a garrison of Gentile soldiers. Between them, seen only by eyes that belonged to the unseen, was a wall. An insurmountable wall dividing Jew and Gentile, having kept them separated since the days of Abraham. Wrestling the wall into his powerful arms, the angel lifted that barrier up, paused before the cross, and waited . . . waited to see crucified upon the cross the dividing wall between the circumcised and the uncircumcised.

He waited, as did the others, for the tick of time to sound once more.

Chapter 42

Arm and hammer began their furious journey downward toward the nail, but not before the returning angels carried their burdens into the bosom of the young
carpenter.

The hammer smashed against the nail, and there
were crucified in that instant

The first man, Adam
Adam's race
The fallen self
The wall of division between heathen and Jew
All governments
Principalities
Powers
Rule . . . and
Dominions.

Yes! *Crucified* upon the cross of our Lord Jesus
Christ!

Chapter 43

Once more a nail was pressed deep into the other wrist. Once more the soldier drew his arm in a mighty upward swing, and once more the Lord froze time and eternity in their journey.

At that very instant one of the angels arrived at the base of Mount Sinai and began to sort furiously through the stones and rocks. He paused. There they lay, smashed, long forgotten. The stone tablets of the commandments and the law of Moses. Quickly the angel clutched them to his bosom, turned, and darted again for Jerusalem's holy temple.

Arriving at the temple courtyard, this same angel went straight into the Holy of Holies. Terrified, yet obedient, he lifted the mercy seat, reached inside the box of hammered gold, and brought forth the sacred copy of the law. He then gathered from within the temple every rule, every regulation, every ordinance that ever had been penned, proclaimed, or dreamed of. *All* law, all legalism, all bondage!

The angel was about to depart when he heard again the Lord's voice within him. Turning, he called forth all ritual of all worship. Once more he would have departed, but turned again at the prodding of his glowing spirit. He now called forth all observance of all holy days. Finally he called forth even the Sabbath.

"You are but pictures of my Lord. Today pictures, types, and shadows of my Lord . . . end!"

At last he left the temple, only to be stopped again. He breathed hard, turned, and called forth even the temple!

"You, too. For even you are but a picture of my Lord. Today the picture ends!"

Now he rose high above the earth, and in a voice that reached all ends of all times, he commanded every rule, regulation, ritual, decree, and ordinance that had ever been observed by any religion ever practiced upon the face of the earth . . . to come forth!

Once more the burdened angel plunged downward through the skies, into time. He arrived just in time to lay his profound burden *into* the bosom of his Lord. He stepped back. "All this . . . ends . . . today!"

The hammer smashed against the nail. And with it,

All law
All rules
All ordinances
All holy days
and
All ritual

were crucified upon the cross of Jesus Christ our Lord!

Chapter 44

The soldiers bound the Lord's legs, pressed them hard against the wood, and nailed his feet to the cross. Ruthlessly they pulled the stake upward, balanced it, and then plunged it into a waiting hole. There was an awful thud and a pathetic groan.

Overhead the heavens were growing dark with some sick and mysterious cloud. Every moment the sky grew darker and more foreboding. Citizens of earth clutched their garments about them and shook inside at the sight of the foulness gathering in the sky above them.

What they saw were but small drops of vast, unholy things seeping through from unseen realms. The angels were now on the darkest and most dreadful of their journeys. Across time and space they flew, into every year, hour, and minute of human history. Into every village, town, and city. Across plain and desert, down even into the seas, they plunged. Rising, they brought back their dreadful cargo to Jerusalem, careful to stay in the invisibles, that they not drown earth with the very stench of their black wares. Darker and thicker grew the massive thing, as numberless angels wrestled to endure their burden until the appointed moment.

The Lord of earth grew faint upon his cross. His time was at an end.

With groans and wails and agonizing cries, the angels lifted their foul booty, stepped into time, and rushed up Golgotha's hill, carrying with them every sin of every man and woman who had ever lived!

Bringing together into one place this vile, pulsating, living thing called sin, they cast it *all* into the Lamb of God—who now became sin incarnate. All sin was now accumulated in one place—*in* him. Divinity now experienced that one thing it had never known. In the flood of that indescribably hideous invasion, the Lord of glory, forsaken of all holiness, cried out in delirium,

My God, my God,
Why hast thou forsaken me?

One of the archangels, blinded with rage and consumed with revenge, cried out savagely to his peers:

Now, now
to that place which is
the last moment of time.
Go, to our enemy! The prince of all princes!
Vengeance, vengeance!
Now, to the ends of wrath.
Vengeance, vengeance upon the damned one.
Go to that last moment

of creation.
Find him! Bring him to the cross!

Once more, to allow for the greatest of all retributions, time stood still.

Chapter 45

Streaking through realms where space and time do not exist, the elect angels flew forward until they came to the ends of creation. And even there, angels found evidence of a cross. With swords raised and with eyes spewing fire, the angels stepped back into time, but a time which was the last second of the existence—in creation—of the kingdom of darkness.

It was Michael who cried out.

Vengeance!
Vengeance!
You—unholy equals—
meet your appointed hour!

Without pity, the elect angels whirled about the dark citizens of demondom—encircling them in fiery, blinding light—and drove them, screaming, back across eternity, back through the portal separating eternity from space-time. Out of the past, the dark host retreated, back toward Golgotha. The *final* moment of time was—at last—about to intersect with the centerpiece of the eternals. Demons of darkness looked up to see that cross, suspended outside creation, and knew by dark instinct they had a rendezvous with this instrument of destruction.

But when this rendezvous? In eternity past, or eternity future? The answer came suddenly enough.

Onward the elect angels mercilessly drove their gnashing, screaming, unholy prey, back toward the cross.

Two archangels with flashing, swirling swords hurled the dark fiends into the bosom of the only begotten Son of God, upon a cross that stood outside all dimensions.

Now went up a defiant cry from the angelic host as has never before—nor ever since—been heard. The whole host of angels and archangels swarmed *again*, into that mysterious portal to find somewhere, in some future place, that fiend of all fiends, and to finish with him a battle that began long ago at the throne of God.

"This time, victory!" they screamed, half mad with rage.

Chapter 46

It was Michael, inflamed with justice, who broke forth in that era that was the *final* moment of this age. There stood the prince of all principalities.

"Before you were created you were defeated. In the eternals you were crucified on the cross of Christ. Now, damned foe, obey my words and go . . . or be driven . . . to that selfsame cross, in time and space!"

Lucifer snarled! But in a fury that matched the wrath of God, Michael drove the infernal angel back through all the ages, stumbling and screaming in full retreat. They stopped at the base of a hill. But not for long. The fire of Michael's unrelenting sword drove the dark prince toward the dying body of the *Lord* of all princes. There Lucifer found himself not only in time, but in a time he quickly recognized as Golgotha, the very place he had once believed to be the sight of his greatest triumph! But no longer did he see the hill as he had seen it before. For an instant he saw the hill through eyes that see things as God sees them. What he beheld now was a cross upon which he had been crucified *before* creation!

By some unutterable means the fallen archangel was drawn inexorably into the very bosom of his enemy.

And so was crucified

*The prince of darkness
and the
kingdom of darkness
upon the cross
of Jesus Christ, your Lord!*

Chapter 47

While time continued its rest, yet other elements of creation gave way to the all-destructive cross and plunged into the Son of God.

While angels watched in amazement, the entire world slipped out of time. That cross, now suspended in a vast realm of nothingness, drove time, space, matter, and eternity into its bosom. Both the visible and invisible creations, the entirety of the cosmological creation, began to melt into the bosom of the Crucified One, disappearing into the young man upon the cross. Time, eternity, and heavenly places soon vanished. The old creation—and all in it that has been diseased by the fall—had passed away!

The eyes of angels, viewing events from *outside* of time, watched as *all things* disappeared.

Before them now stood only a cross, hanging in a great void. All else was gone.

"We are seeing, for one glorious moment, that which the eyes of God have always seen!" whispered the angel who bore the name Recorder.

Truly, he had kept his word. He had put away *all* death . . . *all things.*

Hallelujah!

Chapter 48

A cold chill swept over the angels. They had momentarily forgotten the one last and greatest enemy. That one with whom even they could do no battle.

Death now appeared out of nowhere! Even with creation crucified, the eternal cross had not yet faced that one who boasted of having no enemy except God. There were now only two beings remaining. One had claimed himself to be eternal life; the other claimed to be eternal death, and boasted that by his hand life would die. Death, defiant and fearless, approached the cross and gurgled, in an obscene roar.

We meet again,
and now
for the last time!

Death stretched out his cloak and moved slowly toward his final prey.

The highest drama in universal history had begun!

Yes, Death,
*for the **last** time.*
Delay no longer. Come!

With that, the young carpenter once more moved his blood-soaked, iron-pierced hand. Creation suddenly reappeared. The scene returned to space and time. Earthly things once more came into view. Golgotha reappeared.

The Lord Jesus was now breathing his last breath. The angel of death moved inexorably on, covering the young carpenter with his seraphic wings. Death began squeezing the last breath of life from his final prey.

And Mary's son cried out with his last breath,

> *Father,*
> *into*
> *your hands*
> *I commit*
> *my Spirit.*

With that, the carpenter died, soon to carry with him into the grave all enemies except one. Death, eternally dead, was still alive!

Death watched as life died, and then in a gesture of final victory he threw up his fist and shouted.

> *I have ended*
> *even **Life**!*
> *I am victor*
> *and*
> *conqueror*
> *of all things.*

Death turned to go, darkness radiating from his face in a black, triumphant glow.

Out from somewhere, in a mystery beyond all knowledge, an immeasurable power laid hold of Death.

The black creature turned and screamed, "The Eternal Spirit!" Marshalling all his strength, he brought to bear upon this unseen power a force that caused the angels to drop to their knees in fear.

Angels, who had never dreamed that even one power so great existed, watched two such powers locked in final combat.

For a moment it seemed these powers were equal and that Death might wrest himself free. But slowly, relentlessly, the death angel was drawn toward the still, breathless figure hanging upon that wondrous tree. At last, his strength drained, Azell screamed in horror and disappeared into the bosom of the Nazarene.

And so were crucified *all* things. And such was the death of the Son of God.

Oh, yes.
There was one other thing
placed upon the cross
that day—
you were crucified with Christ.

PART 4

Chapter 49

"We must hurry, Nicodemus. We have no more than an hour."

"But what of the girl? My servants say she is insisting that she be allowed to come here and prepare his body for burial."

"Impossible! It is now only a few minutes before the Sabbath begins. We hardly have time to purify ourselves before the holy day begins. And the girl, despite her devotion, should go and do likewise. It is not proper for her to be handling anything dead on the Sabbath."

"What should I tell her then? Already my servants have had to physically restrain her from coming to your garden."

"Tell her that she may come here on the day after Sabbath and *then* prepare his body for burial. I will instruct the gardener to unseal the tomb for her. But tell her she will need her friends, the other four women; it will be no small task."

Joseph of Arimathea motioned to his servants to begin the burial. They pulled back a huge slab of stone, revealing a very large tomb.

"It is a pity to put him into the tomb . . . this way. It is not a pretty sight."

"But you have allowed him a good place to be buried," replied Nicodemus. "It is a beautiful garden, and only fitting for such a prophet as he to be planted in the ground in such a verdant setting."

At that moment, unseen by any earthly eye, no less than an archangel strolled into the garden and knelt beside the cold, still form of the Son of God. He stared at his side and a wound made by a Roman spear. "Yes," whispered the angel. "Exactly the same place. A gaping hole. And something missing! Only this time *not* a bone!"

The servants surrounded the body of the Nazarene and carefully placed him in the ground . . . as one might plant a lonely, solitary seed.

With that the two men departed the garden, leaving a leaderless archangel to contemplate the scene before him.

"An open side. A singular species . . . one who died without ever knowing a counterpart . . . now cold and still. This lonely one who abode alone for so long . . . has ceased to exist. And now . . . now he is planted in the soil . . . as a *seed?* The earth has become a grave for the Seed of all seeds.

"And what a grave it is. God is buried there! Does no one realize, *God* is buried here! Never has there been such a grave. Buried with him, principalities, powers, all darkness, the enmity between Jew and heathen,

Adam . . . sin . . . all creation! And . . . oh yes . . . one small comfort—Death . . . *he* lies also here entombed!

"No, never has there been such a grave.

"*We* shall wait out our time here," resolved the archangel.

"Out of a scene quite like this, in another garden, came forth a bride for Adam. Kind of his kind.

"Sons of God? Is such a thing possible? *Sons of God? Daughters of God?* Like unto his like? Kind of *his* kind?

"A *counterpart* to our Lord?

"But how?

"It may be—though I know not by what means—this matter shall be concluded *here,* in a fashion worthy of a God who, when he was alive, was ever a bit mysterious and quite prone to the unexpected."

Chapter 50

She awoke with a start. It was that dream again. *Dawn will soon be here,* she thought. *Then I can cease this pretense of sleep.*

Over and over again, in her dreams, she watched him crucified. She was weary and desperate for sleep, but always, the same dream . . . Golgotha!

But *something* in that dream was amiss.

His *side!*

She sat upright.

That was it. His side. The soldier had pierced his side at the moment of his death. She had seen it and screamed in terror. Now she recalled: From the open wound had poured forth blood and water.

"That simply is not possible!" she murmured. "What does it mean?"

She dropped her head and began once more to pour out copious tears from already swollen eyes . . . and wondered how long until the appointed dawn. She lay back down and for a moment drifted off to sleep, only to wake with a cry. It was that dream again.

She would wait no longer. She would go now to

the tomb, while it was still night. The others would know to meet her there. At his grave she might find solace and perhaps even sleep. She slipped out of her bed and reached for the basket filled with jars and vases that she had so carefully prepared the evening before.

A few moments later the young girl stepped out into the dark of Jerusalem's streets, carrying with her the precious aloes, oils, spices, and ointments she would use in preparing her Lord for proper burial. She shuddered to recall that men had callously placed his body into the earth so hastily.

The watchman hesitated only an instant before opening the gate to allow the young girl to depart the city. She paused in the darkness. Her eyes could penetrate the night for only a few feet.

"The hill is in that direction," she said to herself, "as is Joseph's house. And beyond that, the garden."

I worshiped him, I loved him, when he lived, she thought. *He is dead now; but alive or dead, it makes no difference: he is my Lord.*

Down the road she went, then across a meadow to a narrow pathway. Leaving that, she mounted a steep, grassy hill.

Suddenly the earth beneath her feet quivered, jolted, and then shook with a violence. The very planet seemed to be shuddering in the presence of some catastrophic power.

The young girl was flung to the ground. Her basket and its contents were scattered everywhere. She buried her fingers into the grass and held on with all her might. A deep tremble seemed to be coming from the very bowels of the earth, increasing in force as it neared the surface.

Bursting forth at last, the tremor twisted the earth savagely. Chimneys began to fall, roads cracked, and graves split open. The crust of the earth began to roll like an ocean wave. Then came a deafening crack, followed, hard on, by a burst of light. In the midst of this chaotic display of unbridled power, the first small gleam of day made its appearance.

Sunday morning was in the throes of birth.

Chapter 51

The tomb was not spared the onslaught of this strange earthquake, for it, too, reeled in violence. The tomb was, in fact, the epicenter of the quake. No. Not the tomb, but the corpse. Some unearthly power, it seems, had stolen inside that bloodstained body.

All the powers of the Eternal Spirit had met *in* him, there to engage Death in the most titanic struggle of all the ages.

The concentration of energy spiraled, the force of the conflict intensified. Death had died upon the cross, true, but all its powers had frozen an eternal grip upon the soul of its last victim. Earth's foundations trembled in the presence of this struggle to loose Death's unbreakable grip. Creation itself shuddered under the strain while earth released a deep groan, crying out for its redemption. The body of the carpenter reverberated. This Power, whatever it was, was building. The tomb cracked, moaned, and reeled.

For one fleeting instant a soft glow appeared in the tomb, its origin *inside* the lifeless body . . . a momentary foregleam of some enormous force inside him struggling to the surface. One of the carpenter's hands jerked at the upward surge of power from within. There was a burst of light—a light so intense it struck blind the entire heavenly host awaiting without.

All the power and light of eternity had accumulated in one soul and then exploded from out of the bosom of the Son of God—the grave, the earth, the skies, the angels dazzled in a reflected light. For one instant it seemed creation might well dissolve ere the light abated.

The carpenter's body was now engulfed in the purity and holiness of this light. His corpse seemed to disappear in a furnace of liquid radiance. Or had it only *changed?*

Eternal Life had poured out the total content of its power and, in the midst of that explosion, the *form* of flesh had been swallowed up by an eternal and death-less body. A body as spiritual as the Spirit was now blazing from within him!

Now came a thunderous shout . . . from within the tomb!

"I am alive!"

Instantly, without thought or instinct, this man rising out of the sleep of death—like the first man Adam had done before him—grabbed his side.

"A scar! A scar on my side!

"Something is *missing* from *me!* Something . . . someone . . . that has been inside me for all eternity is now missing!"

He rose up *through* the grave cloth, sprang to his feet, and flung off the headpiece.

"Divisible! I have become divisible.

"She who was hidden *in* me for all eternity . . . she has come forth from my side.

"Bone of my bone . . . flesh of . . .

"Nay!" he roared. "Spirit of my Spirit, life of my Life . . . essence of my Essence," he exclaimed, raising both arms high above his head in exultation.

It is true, you see, that if one should thrust his hand into the earth, he will surely bring forth earth. And if one should thrust his hand into the side of man, he will surely bring forth humanity. And, perchance, should one thrust his hand into the side of God, he will surely bring forth divinity!

Something of God had come forth from God, just as surely as something of Adam had come forth from Adam. As Eve was the substance of Adam, so was someone, somewhere, the substance of *him*.

Ironic, is it not, that the singular, most perfect creature in all the universe—standing there in a translated body radiating all the light of the glory of God—had upon his side . . . *a scar!* The evidence of the price he had paid for a counterpart.

Now he raised his hands and face in triumph, and roared, "Where are my rivals? Where are my enemies?"

As was the seed,

so was I,
alone.

Into the earth
I fell
and died.
As did the seed,
so did I.
The Seed
has risen—
I am now risen
and am no more
alone.

First, but
a vision
hidden in
my heart,
now, out of this grave,
my counterpart!

He roared again,

"Her suitors and enemies? Where are her enemies? The damnation that infested the creation . . . where is it?"

The brightness of God billowed forth from him as cataracts of torrential light. For one instant he stood, not in a tomb, nor on earth, but outside the boundaries of eternity . . . God . . . an eternal man . . . crucified . . . risen . . . triumphant over all things.

He cried out in a voice that reached across the boundaries of all creation,

All things are under my feet!
I am RISEN!
Alive forevermore
I am risen from the grave.
Hallelujah!

Chapter 52

He turned and walked through the stone slab; for though his body was still physical, the *physical* of *this* man now belonged to the *spirituals!*

The assembled host of heaven had for three days awaited him. In the garden, upon the hills, round about Jerusalem, as far as unseen eyes could see, the innumerable citizenry of the other realm had waited.

As he stepped forth through the rock, a dazzling fire of liquid light engulfing him, the legions of elect angels broke forth in a wild delirium of praise.

Some of the angels soared, others knelt, most shouted, a few simply flailed their arms. A smaller number jumped up and down. It is even reported—though not confirmed—that some hugged one another, and danced about most unangelically.

One of the archangels, then another, rose into the air and arched about the throng in an enormous circle, leaving a trail of sparkling light in their flight. Soon the entire host joined in this heavenly display, circling about the risen Lord, a veritable tornado of whirling light.

The Lord over Death signaled to the two archangels. Quickly they came and rolled back the door of the tomb, revealing, for all eyes to see, the emptiest tomb on all the face of the earth.

Once more, angels quite beside themselves with joy turned jubilation into chaotic praise.

The Lord signaled for silence, and, though they were never so willing to obey him as now, the praise would begin to subside only to soar again, boiling over to new heights of thunderous adoration. At last the heavenly host fell silent.

A look of defiance had been steadily growing upon the face of the Lord, a thing that seemed somehow almost inappropriate for such a moment. He turned and looked back at the empty tomb, his eyes blazing with the brightness of a thousand infernos.

The Lord lifted his hand again. At some silent command of its Creator, the garden began to fade, as did hills and valleys, sky and stars. All creation seemed to evaporate. Suspended in a vast realm of nothing, there was now nothing present. Nothing save the angels, their Lord, and a tomb.

Every angel knew they were *not* at Jerusalem, nor were they in time. The angels stood, they were certain, either at a time before creation or in some far-future age that would exist after this creation had disappeared and been forgotten.

"What is it I see?" wondered Michael.

"The cross, unbound by creation, existed before

creation, in creation, and beyond creation? It is eternal! So also is the emptiness of the tomb and the triumphant resurrection of our Lord. What does this mean? What is the fate of those things crucified with him, for they were crucified outside of and beyond the effects of time."

Michael knew he would soon have his answer, for his Lord was about to speak.

I have risen from you, O grave.
Now, world, with all your glitter,
you were buried with me.
Now, of your own power, come forth!

There followed the thunder of silence.
Once again he spoke.

Principalities, powers, rulers, and dominions—
you who held sway over man
and held him captive to your system,
you who boasted and flaunted that power—
you were crucified with me!
Now if you can, come forth!

Regal silence reigned.

Prince of darkness—you who
vied for my throne,
you who would have ruled creation,
here, in the eternals,
I declare to you
that which you do not yet know in time:

you were placed in my bosom
and shared this tomb with me—
now of your own vaunted authority, come forth!

Silence fairly screamed in reply.

Now the Lord roared with a passion that unnerved the heartiest angel.

Death—you, the final victor
in all earth's dramas,
you, with a power unrelenting—
by that vaunted power,
greater than all others combined,
Death,
of your own power
live!
Death—damned Death—by
your *power,*
RISE!

A moment of unbearable silence ensued, while angelic eyes strained to see what would come of such defiance.

Nothing moved!

"Know then, Azell, angel of death, you have died! One day, in time, you shall rue the hour you came for my life. When you approached my cross, you swept your sickle across the ages of men, where you harvested with your blade! Creation and all in it have vanished forever. By my cross and by this tomb you have passed away."

Grave . . . where is your victory,
Death, where is your sting!

Creation and all in it had truly vanished forever, vanquished by a cross and a tomb.

The Lord and angels broke forth in spontaneous chorus. Surely the angels would have done themselves harm if they had not given vent to the praise that was welling up from within them . . . except that the Lord brought them to stunned silence as he declared:

"And now, at long last, I will reveal to you—from ages unknown—the *Mystery* hidden in God!"

Chapter 53

The Mystery! There were angelic legends of such a thing. The angel Recorder had whispered of it. But none knew of its meaning nor its content.

A mystery utterly hidden, for it was hidden *in* God.

Once again the Lord raised his right hand.

A great rend appeared in the fabric of the nothingness that surrounded them. What the angels saw within the strange portal was *time* . . . moving *backward*. There was Moses, then Noah, Adam's tragic fall, the creation of man, the creation of earth and stars.

Then rose before their eyes a backward chronicle of eternity—the creation of the angels, an event they all remembered, for it was the *first* of all their memories. Then back to the creation of the *first* angel, Recorder. Then that moment when a limitless God enfolded himself and entered eternity. And then in the backward flight of universal history . . . even eternity ended!

The angels watched spellbound as a scene appeared before them that antedated even eternity's dawn.

They beheld—for the first time—God in his unlimited state. God, the All, *before* all things! Not even in the wildest imagining of their spirits could they have conceived of a God so utterly without limit, so vast, so powerful, so all-encompassing. They were seeing their Lord God *before* he enfolded himself and entered that small realm called eternity. They were seeing God as he *really* is! Some dropped to their knees; others, knowing not what to do, covered their eyes in the presence of such revealed glory.

Somehow, this incredible vision was beginning to change. The angelic host was being allowed to see *the very center* of God.

The idea of a mystery had momentarily slipped from them. But now the purpose of this unveiled vision came to them with stunning suddenness. They were peering into the very center of the depths of God. Yet not one among them could conceive of what mystery lay hidden there.

The scene before them grew brighter; great shafts of sparkling light and storms of flashing brightness emerged. Then, at the very core of this ocean of Godness, *marked off* portions of his being began to become evident. And move.

Something was there . . . hidden in the very center of God.

Somehow the angels grasped that they were seeing that very instant, far back in that pre-eternal age, when their Lord was marking off portions of his being for some high and future purpose. Portions of his being, destined . . . *before* the foundation of the ages . . . for what? They waited. The *marked off* portions of God soon numbered in the millions.

The scene was, somehow, changing again! Every angel felt as if he were seeing something familiar, yet he knew not what! Those marked-off portions of God were glistening like . . . an indescribably beautiful . . . what? A city?

"I thought for a moment I saw a city! For certain, a form of some kind is emerging from the brightness of the light."

That *something*, was becoming a *someone!*

One startled angel, comprehending the first hint of what was gradually forming before their eyes, cried out in shocked amazement.

"Jeru!"

The form continued changing, coming into ever-sharper focus.

Throughout the angelic body could be heard repeated again and again, "Not Jeru, at all, but Eve. Eve . . . it is Eve."

Still the form grew in beauty and in glory. Ten thousand times ten thousand angels fell to their knees, struck down as one, by beauty alone.

There were cries of glory, shouts not unlike sobs, and unprecedented weeping. Some covered their faces, while others raised their hands in exultation.

"More than Eve! Far more than Eve!"

Every angel was now remembering that unforget-
table moment when, during the creation of Eve, the
glory of God overwhelmed all creation. It was a thing
that, until now, they had never understood. Now they
knew! When the Lord created Eve, he was "seeing"
someone else. He had fashioned Eve in the image of an
exotically beautiful woman who belonged to some
other dimension.

That woman now stood before them. There was no
question, Eve was but the foreshadowing of *this one*.
Before them stood a woman of incomparable glory and
beauty, made up of unnumbered millions of portions of
God's own being—portions of God chosen, before the
foundation of the ages, to be the composites of her
being.

Here, at last, was the Mystery *who* had been hidden
in God!

Angels hardly dared to look upon such terrible
beauty, yet they dared not do otherwise.

Here was a woman, robed in the very brightness
and glory of God, with a beauty defying their comprehension. She was like *him*, yet female! A loveliness so
tender, a countenance so full of love, a being so pure
that angelic eyes shone with awe and terror seeking to
take it in. She had been formed out of God. She did not
belong to creation, for he is uncreated. And, as Eve was
bone of Adam's bone, this woman was spirit of the
Lord's Spirit. The uncreated God had revealed to them

his counterpart. A woman fashioned out of the water and spirit of an uncreated God, being of his being.

Her hair was black as ravens, her youth had once inspired a creating God to fashion springtime. Her features encompassed all the beauty of every race and tribe and kindred of womanhood from all ends of creation, for each of them had been but a portion, a picture, of her.

Mercifully, the vision of the glorious woman began to recede. Once more there appeared before the angels the scene of the All of God. Exhausted, angels fell prostrate upon their faces.

"No suitors, no rivals, no enemies," one whispered.

"The mother of Eve," responded another.

"A new Jeru," declared yet another in soft delirium.

One of the angels stood, still half blinded by glory, and uttered, "A counterpart for our Lord!"

"The bride of God!"

"We saw her for but a moment. When will this woman, not formed of things created, not belonging to the fallen creation of the old heaven and the old earth . . . when shall she fully appear before us?"

The answer was evident to all. When the last scene of an already crucified cosmos passed in its forward journey through space and time and the last tick sounded in the continuum of time, when absolutely all that God created in those six days of creation had forever vanished, *then* would this girl, who *is* the *new* creation . . . then would she appear before them.

"Then," whispered one of the archangels, "when there is nothing but the new creation, made up only of things uncreated . . . *then* there will be a wedding!"

Chapter 54

While still intoxicated by glory, the angels began to stagger to their feet. Not one would have dreamed there was yet more to this unveiling.

The resurrected Lord moved toward this pre-eternal scene that he had unveiled before his angels by means of a rend in the fabric of creation. At the same moment the vision of the All of God, out there in pre-eternity, seemed to be moving *toward* the carpenter!

That endless sea of God now poised at the edge of the portal they had been peering into. It seemed the All of God was about to pour out of past eternity into time and space. The Lord Jesus, in turn, moved closer to the portal . . . paused, then raised his hand. That limitless divinity, seen until now only as a vision, broke through the Door separating the two ages and began pouring into the visible realm, into time, into space!

The angels gasped.

The All of God was flowing out of that age which was *before* the ages and was pouring *into* the Son of God! The angels, one and all, considered shielding their eyes,

but one and all decided to choose blindness over missing the sight of this awesome phenomenon.

The Lord Jesus began to glow, his brightness *in this
realm* growing until it matched the brightness of the All
of God in that age before the eternals. Could the All of
God—unlimited—be contained inside the body of a
man? Such a thought was beyond angelic imagination!
Yet, he was, after all, a resurrected Lord—abiding in a
translated body.

The scene became more incredible as the ends of a
now endless God continued sweeping into the Lord of
Lords.

Still the infusion continued until the *very center* of
a pre-eternal God came once more into view. The *center*
of the All of God began to pour into the Nazarene! Now
even those portions of God—marked off in him before
the foundation of the ages—began to move toward
Christ Jesus. The mystery was about to pour into the
Nazarene. The mystery was about to be hidden in *him!*
The Lord lifted his hand once more. The forward flow
of divine life paused. By some amazing power, the
carpenter reached forth through the Door and drew
into his hand the very *first* portion of divinity that had
been marked off in God so long ago! Plucking this light
of Life, he held it high in his hand for the angels to see.
It glistened like diamond fire.

Once again the totality of the All of God resumed
its plunge into the bosom of the Son of God. The forward flow came to an end. The All of God was now in

Christ Jesus. That which was marked off in God before creation's foundation was now *in* him. That woman was now in him as ever she had been.

Suddenly the angels realized this vision had been allowed them so that they might understand the riches that had always been hidden in Christ Jesus. For one dazzling instant the brightness of the All of God shone forth—a torrent of living light—from *within* the Nazarene. The brightness was too intense, too exquisite for any eyes to see fully. Angels, eyes drowned in glory, reached out their hands trying to sense what their blinded eyes could no longer see.

Gradually the light began to fade from their view, as it slipped yet deeper inside the Son of God. At last the glory in angelic eyes began to recede. They could see again.

The Lord of all this glory stood there, alone. He was holding in his hand that *first* dazzlingly bright portion of marked-off divinity. Every angel of heaven knew *that* portion of God had been destined for some incredibly special purpose.

In their seeing of this imponderable vision, they had beheld eternity past and eternity future. As it had been three days before, they had been allowed to see things—such as their enemy, the prince of all principalities—crucified. Now they would have to return to space-time. But in the same moment they were certain that their God—the I AM—remained free of *their* limitation. To him the dissolution of the fallen creation, and all that was in it—had already taken place. They were looking at a Lord who was even at that moment *in* the new creation and who was viewing all things from that vantage point!

Each angel sighed a sigh of disappointment. They were about to return to that lesser place where reality was not so easy to see. They were returning to the confines of space-time. The tomb, which had dissolved from view when this vision commenced, now gradually began to reappear. The hills round about Jerusalem came once more into view. The morning sun was shining brightly in the sky.

While they had been peering into that age past, a few minutes of time had been allowed to pass there in the garden. Every eye of every angel fixed itself on that brightly burning element of divinity the Lord still held high in his hand.

Why was he doing this? Surely the very end of the Mystery was about to be known.

Chapter 55

"We are back in time and space," declared one of the angels. "Yet that woman we saw . . . do you realize that even as we stand in this temporal creation, *she* is *in* him?"

"Yes, and he—like Adam—now has an open side from which can come his . . . counterpart . . . into time, into space!"

"Is that possible?" interrupted another. "We stand in the old, fallen creation. The new creation has not begun."

"Do not be certain," chimed in another. "I remind you of what you witnessed upon the cross and at the tomb. *That* creation has been put away! In *his* eyes, from where *he* stands, it is over."

"So, be certain of nothing when speaking of *his* way," interrupted yet another angel. "And besides, unless I have missed it all, *she* is the new creation!"

"Attention, now, for he speaks again!"

In the most formal and human of ways the young carpenter mounted a stone near the center of the garden and motioned for silence. The bright, glowing portion of divinity was still in his hand and was being held above his head.

"Long ago I declared that I would never create again. But upon my cross that creation, that *old* creation of which I spoke . . . *passed away!*

"I shall now fashion a *new* creation! I shall begin that new creation here. My new creation is beyond the tomb and is *one* with my resurrection . . . *now!*"

What news this was for an angelic host—long saddened by daily watching a creation that had gone so completely astray from its original intention. This was, in fact, what they would, from this day forward, refer to as "the good news."

A grand "Hallelujah" rolled across the heavenly assemblage.

"But when I speak of creating a new creation, imagine not orbiting planets, endless galaxies, nor even heavenly realms! *That* was the *old*. The inauguration of my new creation will be none of those. Nor shall I create a thing *material;* nor shall I even create anything spiritual.

"I shall not *create* at all."

Revelation swept across the faces of the angels. The Lord's words (unlike his ways) were rarely mysterious.

"I shall not create at *all.* I shall *build.* I shall fashion . . . out of my own being the many parts of my new creation. One day I shall assemble these parts into one whole. But I *cannot* create the new creation. This new thing that I began this day is composed of that which is uncreated!

"The firstfruits of my new creation shall be built out of my *own* nature! My essence. My being. My *life*. The first of my new creation shall be built out of *me!* As I formed Eve out of Adam's flesh . . . as I built her out of Adam's bone . . . even so shall I form the new creation out of my own Spirit. I shall build the new creation out of my very being."

A murmur of awe rippled across the angels. The riddle, at last, was solved.

"As I built Eve out of the bone of Adam, bone of his bone, flesh of his flesh, so shall I build my counterpart . . . spirit of my Spirit . . . life of my Life.

"This woman shall be composed of many portions of my being. Not in one hour, nor even in one day, shall I form her. But today I will *begin*."

"*Another* mystery," thought the angels.

"As surely as I rose *this day* from the grave . . . so she also shall rise—this day—from that selfsame grave. She was in me, and today she rose from the grave . . . with me! Today, in the presence of an open tomb . . . today, the day of my resurrection, marks the *beginning* of that new creation!

"Now look to the tomb!

"From out of that tomb shall come the very *firstfruit* of that creation. Today, I *commence* the greatest of all deeds. Today I *begin* the creation, nay, the *building* . . . of my bride! What you are about to see is but a faint miniature of what I will continue to do until the completion of time. I will build a new creation even in the presence of the dissolution of the old, to demonstrate my manifold wisdom and to shame my enemy!"

The angelic assembly found themselves in a state of pure confusion, compounded with elation.

"Look to the tomb!" cried the Lord, holding high the portion of *life* within his hand.

Not until they turned to look at the tomb did they realize, in amazement, that something—no, *someone*—was *in* that tomb.

Chapter 56

Gradually the earthquake began to subside. The frightened young girl raised her head. All around her was evidence of a violent upheaval; even the ground where she lay was rent with fissures. Rising to her knees, she began to gather up the precious ointments that were scattered about.

Fear, doubt, and wonder gripped her heart as she rose and began walking toward the garden. Her footsteps slowed. A strange and powerful foreboding descended on her. For a moment she simply stood, staring transfixed at the garden entrance. Closing her eyes, she pushed open the door. Slowly she moved toward his tomb, dread in every step. There, in the semidarkness of morning, she spied the open tomb.

"Oh no!" she cried. "They have taken him. They have taken the body of my Lord! It is gone. It is gone!"

For a moment the young girl could only stand in horror. Then she turned and began running, crying all the while, "Peter! I must tell Peter! Surely I can find Peter. He hides, I know not where. But I will find him. He will know what to do."

And surely she did find Peter, hiding with another of the disciples. To them she reported her wild story.

They would go and see this incredible thing.

At the garden door, John broke into a run. Peter ran after him. Arriving at the tomb's entrance, John stood there, dazed. Peter pulled him aside and went in. A moment later he staggered out, more insensible even than John.

"Please, please, I know the danger, Peter, but you must go to the authorities. You must find out where they have taken my Lord's body."

"My life may be the forfeit, but I *will* find out," replied Peter soberly.

The three turned from the tomb, their destination, the authorities. But after a few steps the young girl turned.

"No, I will stay. Perhaps Joseph or one of his servants—perhaps the keeper of the garden . . . someone—will return here. If I have news I will come to you. If you have news, *please* send someone to me."

Peter nodded. "Whatever you wish. Follow your heart, as, toward him, you always did."

The young girl returned to the tomb. She knelt at its entrance and, motionless, stared inside.

A strange desire began to grow in her heart . . . the desire to go *into* the tomb. Cautiously she moved through the door and took in the scene: the shroud, the head cover, the very place where he had lain. She was overcome. The young girl fell to her knees and began to

weep. Tears of sorrow, cries of agony rose from a shat-
tered heart. On and on, quite uncontrollably she wept,
until at last, merciful sleep fell upon her.

It was a sleep so deep it seemed akin to death.

Who is this amazing young girl?

Chapter 57

The angels were in total confusion.

Someone was in that tomb. The resurrected Lord had come forth from that tomb; nothing else had. All else had been put away. Had something, or someone, broken free of the destructive power of the cross?

No, that was impossible. Nonetheless, someone was *in* that tomb! And whoever it was, of this they were certain—that *someone* was quite dead!

The Lord spoke.

"I will show you now the firstfruit of my salvation. I will show you the beginnings of my new creation. I will show you . . ." His voice wavered. ". . . the first *portion* of my counterpart."

"And one day, when the last portion of my being— marked off and predestined before the world's foundation—when *that* last portion of my being has been implanted into the very last person destined to be redeemed . . . then shall there be an assembling. Outside of time, beyond the end of this creation, the assembling together . . . and then . . . oh . . . then!"

But who was in that tomb? This was the question

burning in the spirit of every angel. A bride . . . made up of many portions? Or just a portion of the bride? What could be this "new creation"? An entire creation made up only of the substance and being of God? Had they understood him?

It all seemed quite impossible, especially in the light of the extreme and dire condition of fallen mankind. Yet they had seen *this* creation annihilated. What would take its place?

Their answers, they knew, would soon be forthcoming, because . . . whoever was in that tomb . . . had just stirred!

It was a girl. A young girl. Once a terrible sinner—yes, the worst of the whole lot. And, from within the tomb, *she* was moving toward the open door. She was coming out of the tomb, a harbinger of things unseen.

The Lord held yet higher that portion of his own being, making sure that every angel eye could see. His hand began to move. They stood mesmerized as he placed that bright portion of his being into his wounded side.

His side now glistened in splendrous glory.

The young girl had come almost to the very entrance of the tomb. Her eyes were filled with tears, the light of the morning sun was in her face.

"Gardener?" she said.

The angels stood frozen in anticipation.

Chapter 58

"Gardener?" she said again. She began to wipe her eyes with her cloak and tried hard to peer past the morning's bright sun.

"Where have you taken my Lord's body? Please tell me, and I will go to him and care for him."

She now stood on the very threshold of the tomb's doorway. By now, every angel knew this girl was a symbol of what had happened and what would continue to take place as a result of the resurrection. If the Lord's words had not been misunderstood, *whoever* comes forth from the resurrection of their Lord, that person belongs to the *next* creation and has nothing to do with *this* creation. In another instant that former sinner would step forth out of the grave.

The Lord raised his hand. The angels knew that sight. They expected time, once more, to stand still. But it did not. On this occasion it only *slowed*.

The Lord motioned to his angels to look toward the girl. They gasped. Their Lord was allowing them to see right into her heart.

There, deep inside her, they could see that still,

gray thing, that which had once been the very glory and center of Adam. They could *see* the human spirit of this girl lying dead. The human spirit, dead since the fall of Adam . . . no longer able to function toward the unseen realm . . . the very realm from which it had originally come.

Suddenly, the angels realized! This was the Lord *over* death who stood before them. If *he* had risen from the dead, he was himself the power to *raise* the dead. He *was* Resurrection. *He* could bring to life things dead. Yea, he could even resurrect the human spirit—and make it live again! After all these millenia, could the human spirit . . . live? Again? For the first time that morning they really *believed* he might do all the astounding things he said he would do!

"Eve was *in* Adam," said one of the archangels softly, to give utterance to the thoughts of them all.

The Lord calmly lowered his hand and began to reach toward his wounded side . . . to bring forth something out of his side that was *in* him . . . and *of* him. A portion of that Mystery, of that woman who was inside God, was about to be loosed in time and space. A portion of God was about to be . . .

The archangel, now grasping what was about to happen, spoke again.

"Eve came forth from Adam's side."

The Lord drew forth from *within* his side the very Life of God, blazing in light. He proceeded to cast this very portion of his own Life toward the girl. Yet as he did, by mysteries beyond knowing, the stream of light and Life remained flowing from his bosom, unbroken.

Slowly, the luminous ball of fiery Life approached the girl, making her glow within its radiant glory. Just as that light of Life was about to make flight into her heart, the human spirit—long since dead—ignited into glorious life.

The human spirit *had* risen from the dead!

A shout of joy rose from the angels . . . only to subside quickly in wonder.

The archangel spoke again.

"Eve was bone of Adam's bone. This one shall be spirit of our Lord's Spirit."

Still they could not believe their eyes.

The human spirit, made alive by the divine Spirit, was now melting . . . becoming part of the Lord's own spirit. That Spirit—that Life—now moved *inside* the young girl!

"Essence of his Essence," continued the angelic recitation, as the resurrected spirit within the girl, and the divine Spirit from within him . . . became *one.*

The angels were now beholding grace beyond all bounds of imagination as two spirits melted together into one.

"Eve was joined to Adam and the two became . . . one flesh."

The Spirit of the Life of the Lord had now entered into the young girl! Her whole internal being was ablaze with the light of the glory of God. The Life of

God was in her, and *one* with her! The angels were forced to shield their eyes once more. And the minds of their spirits were filled as much with glory as were their eyes. She had been *in him* before earth's foundation— *now* he was in her.

The two shared *one* Spirit.

The resurrected Lord had become *the indwelling Christ!*

Once more, who is this girl?

Chapter 59

"Such glory," murmured Gabriel to himself.

"The spirit of man alive again. What glory!

"The soul redeemed, and now being transformed into the spirituals. What glory!"

His eyes saddened.

"But the body . . . still fallen. Still so utterly fallen. That poor tragic body of fallen—and redeemed—man. For that body, is there no hope of glory?"

Suddenly Gabriel caught sight of yet something else, something that had been implanted within the young girl.

Gabriel saw *inside* that ball of blazing Life that had just entered the girl, something tiny beyond all infinitesimal measure. Gabriel was now gazing at a *seed!* No! More than a seed. For he could see even *inside* that seed! *Within* that seed . . . waiting for some moment when it would be called forth . . . was a translated body. A body not too unlike the translated body of the resurrected Lord. A body wholly physical, yet wholly spiritual, now encased in an infinitesimally small seed . . . inside the Life of God . . . which was now inside the girl.

Gabriel knew somehow, intuitively, that the seed of that body would remain hidden—and forgotten—inside the bosom of the girl . . . until . . . until when?

"Until," Gabriel spoke only to himself, "until I call forth that seed with the sound of a mighty trumpet . . . with the trump of God. In *that* day, the *last* day, a spiritual body shall burst forth out of that seed . . . burst out and swallow up her present body . . . and mortality shall put on immortality.

"Yes, even for the body, there is *the hope of glory!*"

Gabriel strained to hold his being in control as this thought now overwhelmed him.

Others of the angels were struck dumb when, suddenly, they heard Gabriel, almost beside himself, shout with a shout that almost ruptured the earth.

"Behold, full salvation!

"Behold, the new creation!"

Every eye turned again toward the girl.

She stood in the door of the tomb, covered in a brightness of light not seen since creation. The very purity of God radiated from her like rivers of living fire.

The spirit was alive. Divine Life was in her. Her own spirit was one with his. In it all, the soul had been washed as white as snow and was, even now, being transformed by the Spirit of the divine Life radiating out of the spirit into her soul.

"Behold!" thundered Gabriel. "A human being has become partaker of the divine Life."

"Behold," he cried again, as only Gabriel could,

"standing before you that which has never been before. A new species. *A new creation!*

"Behold *the new creation*. Being of his Being. Essence of his Essence. Life of his Life.

"A new creation, *in* Christ Jesus!"

Pure, exquisite bedlam would have broken out at this point, except that the angels realized the beautiful woman who had stepped out of the tomb—dimming all other lights—was about to speak.

In a moment the Lord would lift his hand again, and time would resume its quicker pace, and eyes would again see only the dull things that those with physical eyes are given to see. But at this moment a woman of breathtaking beauty, robed in the purity, righteousness, holiness—and light—of God, had stepped forth from the tomb.

What did the Lord see in that moment?

A girl. A bride! Young. Spotless. Created, nay, built out of the Godness of God. In *his* eyes, she was perfect. And, in his eyes, all *his* rivals—and all her enemies and suitors—no longer existed.

For one bright moment, *through his eyes*, he saw them as . . . the only two living things. Through *his* eyes he saw her somewhere out in post-eternity standing before him, perfect and complete, the divine love of God beating passionately in her—and that same love beating in him. The triumphant Lord and his counterpart! A glorious bride without spot or wrinkle, washed in the blood of the Lamb.

Through *his* eyes he saw a girl who, like him, had risen from the tomb, beyond death's reach, beyond the reaches of all imperfection. She . . . risen, triumphant over the grave. Death beneath her feet.

This is what *his* eyes saw. *What other eyes may see is of no matter.*

Who is this incredible girl? Do you not yet know?

You *are that girl!*

Chapter 60

"Rabboni! Oh, dear teacher!"

She lunged toward him with an abandon that defied all description. And having reached him she clutched him with all her might.

Up until now she had loved him with all her mind, her soul, and her heart. That is, she had loved him with all her human nature. But now, for the first time, she was also loving him—passionately—with all her spirit! For the first time, the Lord of glory was being loved with the *divine* drive of *the love of God*, a love that, until now, was found only in him.

It was quite obvious to everyone, too, that this young girl fully intended never to let him go.

With a warm laugh he said, "Little one, you must release your hold on me; I must ascend . . . to my Father.

"Now go. Go to my brothers. Tell them—

I am ascending to my Father
*and **your** Father,*
to my God
and
***your** God.*

"But Lord, if I depart this place . . . and if you ascend, then I will never see you again," she replied.

"Little one, little one. Be assured. For now . . . and for all ages, I will not—I cannot—*ever* leave you."

The young girl, her eyes filled with tears, her heart bursting with joy, dropped to the ground and kissed his feet.

A moment later this young girl, who had known only to love him and adore him, left the garden to declare a word she knew full well would never be believed.

The angels watched her depart and whispered among themselves.

"She is not his counterpart, is she?"

"No," was the assured reply.

"Yet, yes!" came an answer just as assured. "She is part of—the *first* part of—his bride."

"His bride, it is so clear now, will be made up of *all* the redeemed."

"But how is that possible?"

"That I know not, but after these three days, are you willing to say it is *not* possible?"

"Did you see?" observed another excitedly.

"See what?"

"I am sure of it. You recall the vision? Remember, for one brief instant, he allowed us to look into eternity past (or was it eternity future?) and see his completed bride. She was beautiful beyond all telling. But did you not see! The young girl . . . as she stepped forth from the tomb . . . her features . . . something of that young girl's features were there in the features of the bride of Christ. I am certain of it."

"That," said another, "is because that young girl is *part of* that bride."

"The wonder of it all!" said yet another angel as he shook his head, almost, but not quite, in disbelief.

"Do you not realize," muttered yet one more angel, in total awe, "do you not realize, his bride has never even *seen* the old creation. She belongs to an age beyond the fallen cosmos, beyond the cross, *beyond* the old creation. She has never seen it, been in it, nor does she even know it! Yet she was redeemed out of it."

"'Tis beyond me. It is beyond us all."

The Lord turned to speak to his angels.

"What you have seen . . . that girl . . . perfect . . . radiating the full riches of my life . . . and a whole creation destroyed on the cross . . . *that* is what I *always* see. No mortal eyes shall behold these things until *that* day. Nor is it necessary that they behold, for these things you have seen are matters bound neither by time nor eternity. It is not necessary that they behold these things, nor experience them, nor even *believe* them.

"These are matters that *are*. They have been established. Nothing can change that. It is only what I *see* with my eyes, and the things I *know*, because I have visited all ages from beginning to end. Only *these things* are of any import . . . and only these things are *truly* real.

"*I know* what truly *is*.

"Yet, one day, she *shall* see. She shall see herself as I see her . . . as she truly is. And blessed are those who, having not seen, *believe!*"

He paused, looked about, and spoke quietly to himself, "A witness to my resurrection must be made also in realms unseen. But I must come here again before earth's evening. There are eleven men who need me.

"Now," said the Lord in joyful tone, "Now, my everlasting companions . . . *to the throne!*"

Immediately the angels swarmed into the skies, each to his own place . . . creating a great, angelic corridor reaching straight up into the heavenlies.

"To the throne!" they cried.

As natural as it was for him to be on earth, and in a body quite visible, the Lord stepped into thin air and, quite naturally, began to ascend through the midst of that angelic corridor . . . into the sphere of the invisible and the spiritual.

But he would not lay off his earthly vestige as he approached the other realm. A *visible* human being was about to make his home in that quite invisible place.

A *man* in the glory!

He threw one hand high into the air and cried again,

To the throne!

And as angels watched the lowly carpenter step through the portal between two worlds they saw, for the first time, a man in heavenly realms. They knew they were declaring his rightful place as they cried out in response:

To the throne—
The ever-living One
The triumphant One
The Lamb of God
The carpenter of Nazareth
The Son of Man
The Son of God
The Lord of Lords
and
King of Kings!

To the throne! To the throne!

The Final Act

Chapter 61

It is evening. A young woman climbs a high hill, throws back her head, and allows her eyes to wade through the starry sky. Her heart is full of love for a Lord she has worshiped and adored for many years now.

She wonders. On how many occasions, by now, has he stopped time, bypassed eternity, reached back into that primordial era, and, in some mysterious way known only to him, plucked from out of the center of his being . . . *his own life* . . . and thrust that life into the bosom of one who had just believed in him?

How many spirits within the bosom of how many men and women have been raised from the dead and ignited into life? How many souls under transformation? Do eons lie ahead before that last portion of God is implanted in the last believer? Or will it be tomorrow?

When will that vast host of the redeemed be lifted out of time and space to discover for themselves that the cross has put a whole creation to death and made a people wholly righteous? When will they see with *his* eyes? When will they know that the history of the bride began *after* all things?

"When shall we know . . . as we are known," whispers the young woman pensively. She, like her God, has never aged. "Oh, but that is an eternal thing. I am in time!" When will she be freed of these temporal bonds, to *know* these things?

"When . . . shall mortality put on immortality? When . . . shall all inhibitions of the flesh fade away? When . . . will *I* know . . . as he has always known me? When . . . spirit return to Spirit? When . . . his day? When . . . her day?

"When will time and eternity intersect . . . when is *fullness of time?* When shall the bride have made herself ready?

"When shall I cast my eyes into these very skies . . . and see angels . . . ten thousand times ten thousand. Innumerable. Descending! When, earth, will you complete your last orbit . . . and I . . . we . . . be plucked from here by his almighty power? Changed. Before the eyelid can wink. Like him! The veil of the *flesh* broken! *Then* shall I see the unseen. *Then* shall I know as I am known.

"And when the wedding feast?" she seems to ask the stars.

"When shall the fiancé become the bride, and the bride . . . the wife?

"Past, present, future shall dissolve into one, *then* disappear! Then I, as part of that bride, shall love him with all the power and passion of my new being!

"How the consummation?"

She looks again into the skies, from horizon to horizon.

A far-off day begins to fill her mind's eye. She begins to see an event far, far distant . . . even *eternity's last moment*. She begins to see. . . .

Chapter 62

What is this emerging scene? Is it that moment, far past, when God was the All?

No. Yet it is like unto it.

Then what vision is it that we now behold?

A Door opens in the new heavens. A great swarm of light begins to descend from out of that realm. This light, it is a city! The *New* Jerusalem. A city of a hundred million shining stones, each glowing with the glory of the light that is its center. And the center is the Lord, Christ Jesus!

The city begins its descent, and as it does, it begins to change. A galaxy of living light it is, swirling downward in the skies. Gradually this stardust of light becomes a multitude of people—that vast host of the redeemed, a multitude no man can number.

They are, as one, offering up jubilant praise to their Lord and Savior. The angelic host surrounds them, and together the two hosts join one another in an anthem, unleashing the mightiest tribute of rapturous praise ever to be known.

Around and around their Lord the angels circle,

while the vaults of a new heaven and a new earth echo the chants of adulation of redeemed man and elect angels.

The scene begins once more to change.

That vast, innumerable throng standing beneath the angels and before the Lord begins to flow together, becoming, at first, one great light of lights. The brightness grows, the lights become all *one.* At the center of this light, a form begins to emerge.

The angels exult in holy delight. They recognize that form, for they have seen it once before in a brief moment of glory . . . long ago on the day of his resurrection.

Standing before them is the Bride of the Lamb.

She emerges into clear view, the radiance of her light and glory eclipsing all save the throne of God. She stands before them robed in purity and holiness.

The angels bow with a gentleness and tenderness never before displayed. She is, once more, the reality of the picture. All the loveliness of all womankind is sculptured into one beauty, resting upon *her.*

An innocence flows from her that enraptures even the holy angels. Her eyes have never seen or known one glimpse of the tragedies that befell the old creation. She stands there in the strength and perfection of youth. Her raven hair, her glowing visage tell a thousand tales of love, of passion, of singular devotion to her Lord. A majesty, a grandeur, and an exalted beauty radiate from her as terrible as the face of God.

For a moment all things else seem to vanish away in the presence of this holy and glorious bride. Suddenly, though, there appears in the distance a yet greater glory.

None else but the King!

The woman begins to glow with a brightness far beyond the ends of belief. The glory of the brightness of the Lord ignites with a fire that immerses—and then consumes—all else. And from within this sea of endless glory . . . arises a shout!

> *Forever!*
> *No more*
> *alone.*

As two gleeful children might, they run toward one another and embrace in an exchange of divine love. With all else having already dissolved, the light of the glory of the two now melts into one.

Long ago the Lord gave up his unconfined endlessness and enfolded himself into that smaller place called eternity. Now, one with his bride, he releases himself back to his true and endless expanse.

Has he, then, become—once more—the All?

Nay, but rather, he has at last become that which he purposed to become, there, before the foundation of the ages. He has become

The All in all.

Chapter 63

The distant vision begins to fade, then it vanishes.

The young woman, now standing at the crest of an emerald hill, rises to her feet, a deep sense of the love of the Lord stirring within her . . . for she has just heard the overwhelming cry of the living Holy Spirit within her.

And that Spirit within her has cried . . . *Come!*

And like Eve before her, she lifts her hands to the skies, raises her voice, believing that her counterpart might hear her . . . and cries:

Come, Lord Jesus. Come!

And just beyond the Door, in realms of glory, he who loves her and died for her . . . now hears her plea.

"At last, she is putting off lesser things, knowledge, service, sacrifice. She is returning to the highest order of the universe.

"She is learning to *love* me," he whispers.

Soon,
yes, soon now . . .
very, very soon . . .

Gabriel!

Farewell

It is late, and we must say good-bye. I trust you have seen something this hour that will forever remain with you and— perhaps—even change *you!*

The players, I am told, are preparing another performance. Their first, as you recall, was a drama. Now this, a love story. The next—I hear—shall prove perhaps to be an adventure . . . an adventure into realms unseen. If I am not mistaken, their next production shall be The Chronicles of the Door. *Ah! Now* there *is a tale for the telling. As the Lord wills, I trust we shall meet again, yet thrice.*

Gene Edwards has written two unique books on the deeper Christian life. If you have a heart to go deeper with Christ, these are among the best and most practical books on the subject available anywhere. They are *The Highest Life* and *The Secret to the Christian Life*.

Edwards continues his allegorical books on the deeper Christian life with the following books, all as powerful and beautiful as *The Divine Romance: The Prisoner in the Third Cell*, and *A Tale of Three Kings*.

The books *The Birth* and *The Beginning* are part of a series called The Chronicles of the Door.

You can reach Gene Edwards at
Message Ministry
P.O. Box 18203
Atlanta, Georgia 30316.